THOMAS JEFFERSON

✺ ARCHITECT ✺

THOMAS JEFFERSON
⋇ ARCHITECT ⋇
THE INTERACTIVE PORTFOLIO

—————— CHUCK WILLS ——————

Running Press
PHILADELPHIA · LONDON

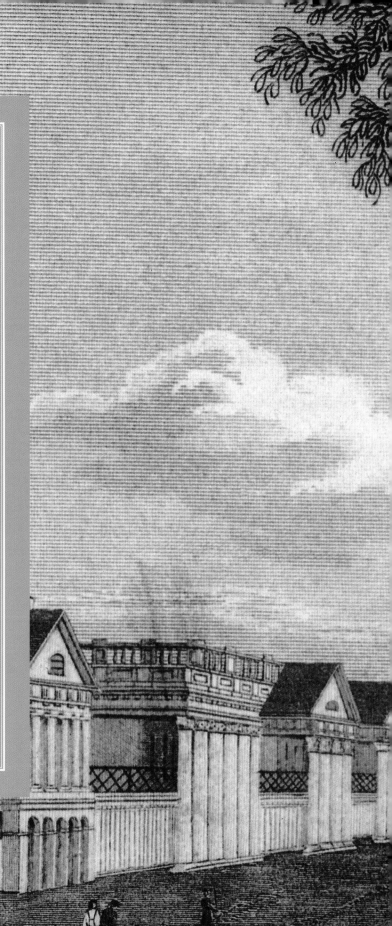

CONTENTS

6   INTRODUCTION
FATHER OF DEMOCRACY, FATHER OF AMERICAN ARCHITECTURE

8   CHAPTER 1
THE EDUCATION OF AMERICA'S ARCHITECT

20   CHAPTER 2
JEFFERSON'S HOME: MONTICELLO

42   CHAPTER 3
JEFFERSON'S CAPITOL: VIRGINIA STATE CAPITOL

56   CHAPTER 4
JEFFERSON'S RETREAT: POPLAR FOREST

68   CHAPTER 5
JEFFERSON'S UNIVERSITY: THE UNIVERSITY OF VIRGINIA

86   TRANSCRIPTIONS

90   IMAGE CREDITS

91   BIBLIOGRAPHY & ABOUT THE AUTHOR

INTRODUCTION
FATHER OF DEMOCRACY, FATHER OF AMERICAN ARCHITECTURE

On April 29, 1962, President John F. Kennedy hosted a state dinner for Nobel Prize laureates at the White House. "I think this is the most extraordinary collection of talent, of human knowledge, that has ever been gathered together at the White House," he said, "with the possible exception of when Thomas Jefferson dined alone."

Few Americans accomplished so much in so many disciplines as Thomas Jefferson. He was, of course, a great statesman: author of the Declaration of Independence, first secretary of state, two-term president, prime mover behind the Louisiana Purchase and the Lewis and Clark expedition. He's also justly celebrated as a diplomat, agronomist, inventor, writer, philosopher . . . the list goes on.

And yet, curiously, Jefferson's greatness as an architect wasn't clearly understood until the second decade of the twentieth century. Biographers and historians knew about his Virginia home, Monticello, and they acknowledged his involvement in the creation of public buildings like Virginia's Capitol at Richmond and the "Academical Village" of the University of Virginia at Charlottesville. But they usually presumed that the designs of these structures were derivative and/or the work of others.

That finally changed when a young architectural historian, Sidney Fiske Kimball, and his wife, Marie Goebel Kimball, discovered a trove of plans for Monticello written in Jefferson's own hand in the archives of the Massachusetts Historical Society. The publication of Fiske Kimball's *Thomas Jefferson, Architect* in 1916 sparked new interest in and appreciation for Jefferson as an architect that continues to this day.

Jefferson's architectural vision evolved over his long life, but it was always coherent. One could sum it up as "back to the future." "Back," in this case, means the buildings of ancient Greece and Rome. Jefferson first encountered these as a young man via Italian Renaissance architect Andrea Palladio's *The Four Books of Architecture* and the "pattern books" of Palladio's British disciples, and later he saw some of the original structures during in his travels through Europe. In the architecture of antiquity, Jefferson found architectural forms that he believed were appropriate for a new, self-created nation that drew on the examples of Greek democracy and the Roman Republic for its political forms. "Jeffersonian Classicism," as it came to be called, was also a kind of architectural declaration of independence; it was an explicit rejection of the English-derived architecture predominant in colonial America.

As to the "future," Jefferson did far more than copy classical models; he adapted them to the settings and materials of his native land and added individual touches from his amazingly vigorous intellect. Physically and philosophically, Jefferson's architecture faces forward. Monticello is the classic example; it may resemble a Palladian country house, but it's set on a hilltop facing the west, with an interior crammed with time- and labor-saving devices, many of them of Jefferson's own design.

The influence of Jeffersonian Classicism can be seen around the country, from small-town libraries to college campuses to the great government buildings of the nation's capital. It can also be seen in the later work of the highly talented artisans he employed on his various buildings, some of whom became notable designers in their own right and carried on his architectural philosophy.

While it took many decades for Jefferson's architectural contributions to come to light, his status as America's first great architect—and maybe America's greatest architect—is now fully acknowledged. Thanks to his authorship of the Declaration of Independence and his myriad other contributions during the founding of the United States, Jefferson has been rightly called "the author of America," but he can just as accurately be called "the architect of America."

Opposite: Monticello, c. 1994

CHAPTER

1

THE EDUCATION OF AMERICA'S ARCHITECT

1743–1826

> *"Putting up and pulling down is one of my favorite amusements."*
>
> —THOMAS JEFFERSON

Thomas Jefferson was born on April 14, 1743, at Shadwell—a small, simple, wood-frame farmhouse in Albemarle County, Virginia. Surrounded by the fields of tobacco that were the backbone of Virginia's economy, the dwelling stood on the banks of the Rivanna River at the edge of the colony's Piedmont region. He was born on Virginia's western frontier. Like many ambitious young Virginians, Jefferson's father, Peter, had moved his family (and his slaves) inland from the colony's Tidewater region in search of more and better land.

Peter Jefferson was a big man, reportedly able to lift two 500-lb. barrels of tobacco at one time. Thomas Jefferson later wrote that his father's education "had been much neglected," but he recorded that his father "[i]mproved himself insomuch that he was chosen [by the colony], with Joshua Fry, professor of mathematics at William and Mary College, to run the boundary line between Virginia and North Carolina. . . ." So Peter Jefferson was a land surveyor and mapmaker as well as a planter. Surveying, especially in the rugged wilderness of western Virginia, required a high degree of mathematical skill, and some scholars speculate that Thomas's pride at his father's accomplishments inspired his interest in architecture and design.

The Shadwell house is long gone, but it was probably much like the typical Virginia farmhouse of the time,

Left: Example of a typical Virginia farmhouse, built in 1795 *Left, inset:* Engraving of Thomas Jefferson, c. 1780

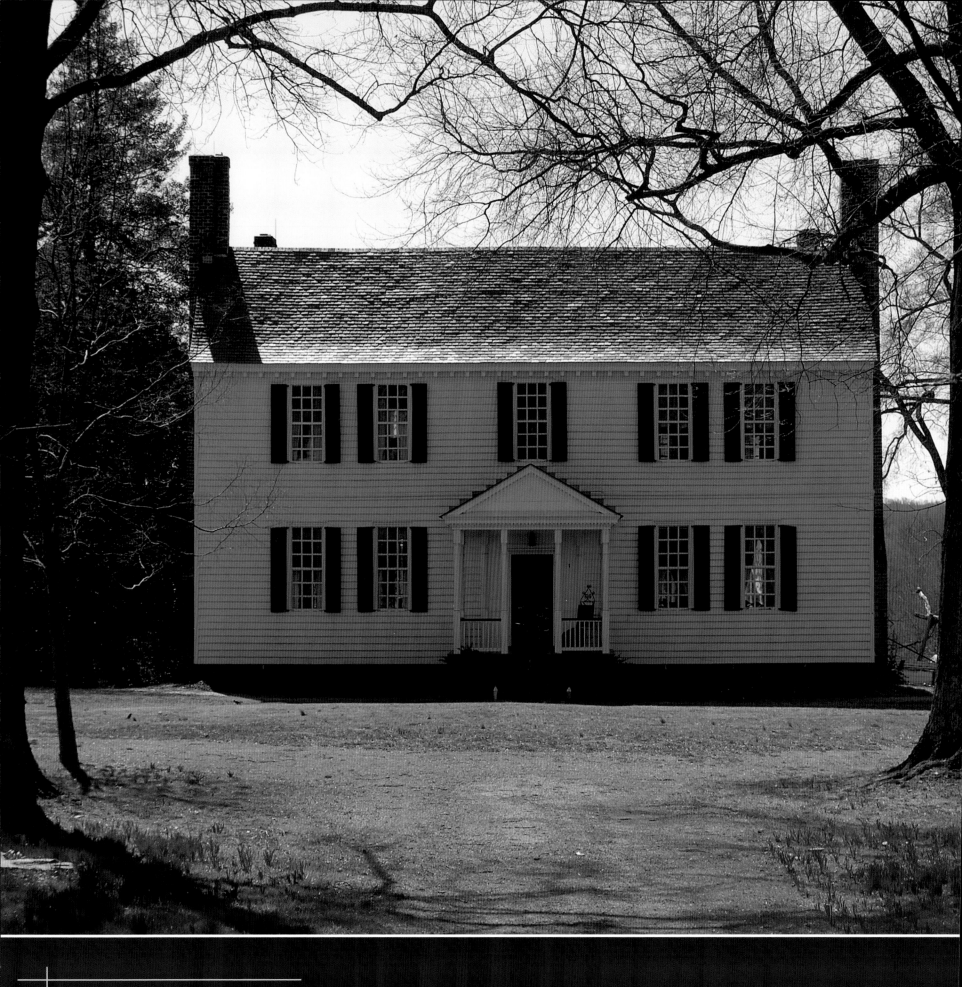

which possessed a parlor for entertaining guests and bedrooms on the second floor. Biographer Willard Randall also describes these homes as:

> [G]abled . . . with a fireplace on each end and a central hallway, front to back, dividing the two main rooms on the ground floor. The passage, as it was called, provided much-needed cross-ventilation during the hot Virginia summers.

Thomas was not yet three years old when the family moved fifty miles away to Tuckahoe, near Richmond. In his incomplete memoirs, he wrote that his earliest memory was the horseback ride from Shadwell to Tuckahoe, propped up on a pillow and held by a slave. Tuckahoe was just one of several plantations owned by the Randolph family—one of the wealthiest clans in the colony.

The move was prompted by the death of William Randolph—a cousin of Jefferson's mother, Jane Randolph, and a close friend of Jefferson's father. On his deathbed, William asked Peter Jefferson to look after the Tuckahoe plantation, and Peter honored his wish.

The main house at Tuckahoe was vastly more spacious and luxurious than Shadwell. Its design and layout likely influenced the home with which the grown-up Jefferson would always be associated—Monticello.

Like most American dwellings of the colonial era, Tuckahoe's design echoed the architecture of Europe—England, in this case. All of the countries that colonized what would later become the United States imported their architectural traditions with them, from the narrow gabled buildings of Dutch New Amsterdam to the houses with their wrought-iron balconies in New Orleans's French Quarter (although the latter were more influenced by Spanish than French houses).

Tuckahoe would not have looked out of place in a rural English shire, but there were concessions to local conditions. In a land where there were plenty of trees but relatively few skilled masons and bricklayers, the house was of wood-frame construction, although Flemish-bond brickwork was incorporated at the ends. (In Flemish-bond brickwork, bricks are laid with their short and long ends alternating in single rows for a decorative effect.) Tuckahoe's covered porches provided an escape from the stuffy interior in the summer.

The original house had been built in the 1720s and later expanded so that the final structure was roughly H-shaped, with two wings containing family quarters connected by spaces for entertaining. Some historians conjecture that young Thomas watched, fascinated, as construction took place on the house—sparking his interest in architecture.

Although the construction itself might have impressed Jefferson, the wood-frame building materials of both Shadwell and Tuckahoe definitely did not. In his *Notes on the State of Virginia* (1781), he wrote:

> [American] private buildings are very rarely constructed of stone or brick, much the greater portion being of scantling and boards, plaster with lime. It is impossible to devise things more ugly, uncomfortable, and happily more perishable. . . . The inhabitants of Europe, who dwell chiefly in houses of stone or brick, are surely as healthy as those of Virginia. These houses have the advantage too of being warmer in winter and cooler in summer than those of wood; of being cheaper in their first construction . . . and infinitely more durable. . . . A country whose buildings are of wood, can never increase in its improvements to any considerable degree. Their duration is highly estimated at 50 years. Every half century then our country becomes a *tabula rasa*, whereon we have to set out anew. . . .

The adult Jefferson's aversion to wooden buildings was also probably fueled by the fact that his boyhood home, Shadwell, burned down in 1770, taking with it his early personal papers and the treasured library he'd assembled as a young man. As Jefferson put it, "I cannot live without books."

Opposite: Tuckahoe's main house *Above:* The H-shaped rear of the main house at Tuckahoe plantation

The Williamsburg Years

Along with his siblings and the young Randolphs, Jefferson first attended school in a little outbuilding on the grounds of Tuckahoe. The Jeffersons returned to Shadwell when Thomas was about nine years old, but for the next seven years, Shadwell was mainly a weekend home for young Tom. In accordance with his father's wishes, Jefferson was packed off to study and live with local private tutors, from whom he learned Greek, Latin, and French. And as with any young Virginia gentleman, Jefferson's education included instruction in the social graces, including learning to dance and to play the violin.

The teenaged Thomas was tall. He eventually topped out at about six feet, two inches—significantly taller than most American men at the time. And he was handsome, with fair skin, a shock of red hair, and piercing eyes, the latter described by various observers at different times of his life as "blue," "gray," or "hazel."

"Tall Tom," as he was nicknamed, arrived in Williamsburg, Virginia at the age of sixteen to attend the College of William and Mary. Virginia's capital in 1758, Williamsburg was a town of about a thousand inhabitants—half of them slaves. It was the first town of any substance Jefferson had lived in, and the first with any public buildings of note—the Governor's Palace, the Capitol, and the college itself.

Above: Gates of the Governor's Palace, c. 1950 *Opposite, top:* The Governor's Palace, Williamsburg, Virginia *Opposite, bottom:* The Wren Building at the College of William & Mary

William and Mary was housed in what was known as the Wren Building, which had been built between 1695 and 1700.

At William and Mary, Jefferson studied hard, sometimes fifteen hours a day. But he also lived the good life, vacationing with classmates at nearby plantations—such as Rosewell, home of his friend John Page and one of the finest homes in the colonies—and spending convivial evenings at the Governor's Palace, which Jefferson himself would one day occupy.

Jefferson didn't think much of Williamsburg's architecture. Most of the grand buildings were designed in the stolid (and sometimes stodgy) Georgian style popular in England at the time.

While in Williamsburg, Jefferson took his first big step toward becoming an architect. Learning that a local cabinetmaker—who was fond of booze and needed money for a bottle—was looking to sell some old books, Jefferson stopped by and bought his first tome on architecture. Exactly which book is still debated. It might have been James Gibbs's *Rules for Drawing the Several Parts of Architecture* or Robert Morris's *Architecture*, both by contemporary English designers. The work could also have been an English translation of *I Quattro Libri Architettura* (*The Four Books of Architecture*) by the sixteenth-century Italian architect Andrea Palladio. Certainly Jefferson encountered *The Four Books* at some point as a young man. He would own no fewer than five editions of the work in the course of his lifetime, and he later described Palladio's book as his architectural "bible."

The Wren Building

Officially known as the College Building, the Wren Building got its name from the belief that its design was the work of the great English architect Christopher Wren (1632–1723), designer of many London churches, including St. Paul's Cathedral. However, the only evidence for this is a single reference in a letter written in 1724 by a William and Mary professor. The original plans—whether Wren's or someone else's—have disappeared. Young Jefferson was no doubt aware of the structure's supposed pedigree, but later in life, in his *Notes on the State of Virginia*, he derided the building as a "rude, mis-shapen pile." In 1772, Virginia's colonial governor gave Jefferson the job of drawing up plans that would have modified the original structure and its grounds, but the coming of the Revolutionary War halted the work.

AMERICAN PALLADIANISM

It's impossible to understand the evolution of Jefferson's architectural philosophy without a detour through the life and work of Palladio.

The son of a miller, he was born Andrea di Pietro della Gondola in Padua—then part of the Republic of Venice—in 1508. He learned the craft of stonecutting as a teenage apprentice and became a skilled stonemason and bricklayer, working in the Veneto (the area surrounding Venice) on the country retreats of the city's aristocracy and on the rural estates of the landed gentry. It was in this capacity that Andrea della Gondola met Count Gian Giorgio Trissino (1478–1550).

The count was the very definition of a "Renaissance man"—a poet, a playwright,

an educator, and an all-around patron of the arts. He embodied the humanist *zeitgeist* of his time—an era in which Europe (with Italy in the lead) was shrugging off the dust of the Middle Ages while looking back to classical Greece and Rome for examples of how to live and create.

Trissino and della Gondola met when the latter was in his early thirties and working as a stonemason on the Villa Trissino, which the count was building to house a kind of academy for scholars in various fields. Trissino quickly recognized della Gondola's talents and became the younger man's patron and mentor, giving him the name Palladio—derived from Pallas Athena, the Greek goddess of wisdom.

At the Villa Trissino, Palladio mingled with the elite of Venetian society, including architects such as Sebastiano Serlio (1475–1554). Here he absorbed the Mannerist style of architecture in vogue at the time, which drew on Roman examples—buildings *all' antica* ("in the antique manner"). But the Romans had left little theoretical guidance for later builders. The only significant architectural treatise that survived from antiquity was *de Architectura* (now usually known as *The Ten Books of Architecture*) by Vitruvius, a Roman architect active in the first century BCE. The first modern edition of the book was published in Florence in the early fifteenth century, and it had a profound effect on Renaissance architecture, on Palladio, and ultimately, on Jefferson. (Palladio also published a popular version of *de Architectura* in 1567.)

In *de Architectura*, Vitruvius argued that buildings must be *firmitas*, *utilitas*, and *venustas*—durable, useful, and beautiful—and that they should be based on the geometric forms found in nature, like the circle and the square, to achieve proper proportions. (Leonardo da Vinci applied Vitruvian principles in his famous drawing of the human form, *"Vitruvian Man."*)

De Architectura covered a wide variety of subjects—from the importance of sightlines and acoustics in designing theaters to the practicalities of plumbing. But Vitruvius's most significant contribution to Western architecture was to identify and classify the styles of the vertical-post/horizontal-beam combinations—columns, as we know them—and their accompanying decorative motifs that comprised the basic structural elements of temples and other public buildings.

In *The Four Books*, which Palladio published in 1570 at the beginning of the last decade of his life and career, he described these "classical orders," as they were known: Tuscan, Doric, Ionic, Corinthian, and Composite. Each of the five orders was suited to a particular kind of building—the fairly plain Tuscan, for example, was good for barns and other simple structures, while the more ornate

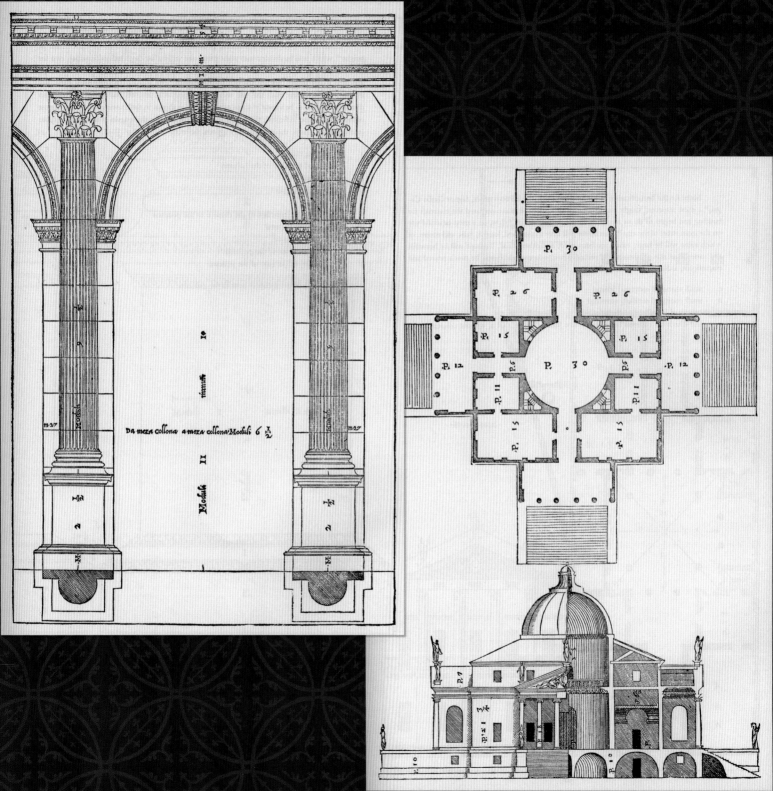

Da meza collona a meza collona Moduli 6 ½

Moduli II

Corinthian and Composite were suited to grand houses and public buildings. The Vitruvian/Palladian orders essentially gave architects of the Renaissance and beyond a fundamental grammar to draw upon for their designs. The section of *The Four Books* that dealt with the classical orders was so popular it was often published as a stand-alone volume.

To understand how to best apply these concepts in practice, Palladio, the budding architect, had to become an archaeologist. In the 1540s, he and Trissino visited Rome, where Palladio measured and sketched what remained of the city's ancient temples and other structures. Back in the Veneto, Palladio began to build in the style that would eventually bear his name. It should be noted that despite being deeply influenced by classical architecture, Palladio wasn't just copying ancient designs; in an architectural historian's phrase, he "filtered" the buildings of antiquity through his own vision.

Palladio made important contributions to Renaissance church design, but his great gift was for designing residences—what's known as "vernacular architecture."

His designs included both *palazzos* (palaces, or town houses) for Venice's urban elite and *villas* (country homes) for the landed gentry of the countryside.

The Palladian style is best expressed in his villas. They stood in contrast to the ornate style of the late Renaissance. Inside and out, the emphasis was on proportion, balance, and symmetry; the whole structure and the rooms within were often based on mathematical ratios. Built largely of brick and stucco, the basic template of a Palladian villa was the classical temple, with a columned façade topped by a triangular gable, or pediment.

The façade gave the impression that, like a temple, the interior was a single large space, but the interior usually comprised three stories. The first was a ground floor for service rooms, often rusticated—set partly belowground. The main floor, or *piano nobile*, was accessed via a set of steps and through a central *portico* (porch); it contained the "great rooms" for entertaining and the family bedrooms. The third floor, or *mezzanine*, housed more bedrooms and servants' quarters. Wings flanking the main structure had the practical benefit of housing the kinds of workspaces required

Opposite: Drawings from Palladio's *The Four Books*: Corinthian columns (top); the plan for the Villa Rotunda (bottom) *Above:* Villa Rotunda, Vicenza, Italy

by a country estate—storerooms, workshops, and the like. The wings also anchored the main structure to its natural setting, while simultaneously promoting a sense of symmetry. Large windows brought abundant light into the interior—and although he didn't invent the style, the kind of arched window used in Palladio's houses is still known today as a "Palladian window."

Palladio also paid close attention to the natural settings of his houses. They were usually sited on a hill to provide the villa's inhabitants both with a view and with cooling breezes during the summer. Similarly, the villa's central portico was often flanked by *colonnades* where the villa's dwellers and their guests could stroll in the open air.

The Palladian style began to spread outside of the Veneto when translations of *The Four Books* appeared throughout Europe following Palladio's death in 1580. The work wasn't translated into English until 1715, but by that time the style had been imported into England by Inigo Jones (1573–1652), who saw Palladio's buildings firsthand while traveling in Italy. They deeply influenced his designs for a royal residence: the Queen's House in Greenwich (begun in 1616, completed in 1635) and the Banqueting House at Whitehall (begun in 1619, completed in 1622).

Palladianism didn't really take off in England and Ireland until the eighteenth century, when members of the aristocracy commissioned country houses in the style; Wilbury House in Wilshire (1710), built by William Benson, a wealthy member of Parliament, is thought to be the first example of this "Palladian Revival" or "Neo-Palladian" style in England. By the time Jefferson became acquainted with Palladio, though, the style was falling out of favor in England, supplanted first by Baroque designs and later by the Neoclassical style.

It's little wonder that Jefferson became Palladianism's American champion. Its classical roots certainly appealed to him. Like all well-off, learned Americans of his generation, Jefferson's education was steeped in "antient" (Jefferson's occasional spelling for "ancient") writers; he would have been as familiar with Horace's *Odes* or Virgil's *Aenied* as with Shakespeare's plays and John Milton's poetry. Like the other men who fought the Revolutionary War and established the United States, he was inspired by the example of the Roman Republic, with its emphasis on "civic virtue" and resistance to tyranny. The designs of Palladio and those he influenced were, in a way, an architectural legacy of these qualities.

Jefferson was also very much a man of the Enlightenment—the eighteenth-century intellectual movement that championed freedom of speech, religious toleration, scientific inquiry, and a rational approach to life. One of the key concepts of the Enlightenment was the idea of "natural law"—that the world was an orderly place in which universal principles could be observed and applied, both in the physical world and in the sphere of human affairs. With its emphasis on mathematically derived proportion and symmetry, and on following fundamental rules of design, Palladio's late Renaissance architecture was still in tune with the spirit of the Enlightenment.

Still, despite Palladio's influence, Jefferson no more copied Palladio slavishly than Palladio himself copied Greco-Roman designs. In the words of his biographer Fawn Brodie, "Jefferson as an architect has been described as a classicist. But this does not mean that he was a conservative." Just as Palladio adapted classical models to his time and place, Jefferson, in his designs, used the spirit of Palladio to infuse a style that was both very personal and wholly American—a style meant for a land that both looked back to the classical past and forward to a future of its own vigorous making.

And the first expression of that style was Monticello.

Jefferson the Gardener

Jefferson's passion for horticulture was on a par with his passion for architecture and invention. He experimented with plants—edible, decorative, fragrant, or otherwise useful—all his life, documenting the results in his *Garden Books*, which he kept for nearly sixty years. A semi-vegetarian—he wrote that he usually only ate meat "as a condiment for the vegetables"—he ultimately oversaw the cultivation of more than 200 varieties of vegetables and a similar number of fruits in the kitchen garden and orchards at Monticello, his principal country home. Jefferson's stint as a diplomat in Europe gave him a taste for plant foods that were unfamiliar in North America—including the tomato (or "tomata," as he sometimes spelled it), which most Americans of his time regarded as poisonous.

Enclosures: Pages from Jefferson's *Garden Books* outlining the growth of various plants, flowers, and vegetables at Shadwell from 1766–1767, and at Monticello in 1768 *Opposite:* Aerial view of Monticello's West Lawn, Main House, Mulberry Row, Vegetable Garden Terrace, and the South Orchard

CHAPTER *2*

MONTICELLO

1768–1808

> *"Mr. Jefferson is the first American who has consulted the fine arts to know how to shelter himself from the weather."*
>
> —THE MARQUIS DE CHASTELLUX, 1782

After graduating from William and Mary, Thomas Jefferson studied law with George Wythe (1726–1806), who became a father figure to the young man (Peter Jefferson had died in 1757); Jefferson would later write that Wythe was "my faithful and beloved Mentor in youth, and the most affectionate friend through life" and "my second father." (Jefferson's relations with his mother were difficult, and he rarely spoke or wrote about her.)

Jefferson was admitted to Virginia's Bar in 1767 and elected to the House of Burgesses, the colony's legislature, a year later. But his heart really wasn't in his law practice, or—at that point—in politics. When Jefferson turned twenty-one, he inherited about 5,000 acres of land (and sixty or so slaves) around what's now Charlottesville in Albemarle County. Here, on a 1,000-acre parcel "patented" by his father in 1735, he began to build what would become Monticello.

In fact, Monticello was really two distinct structures. Architectural historians usually identify them as Monticello I and Monticello II. Sources differ on exact dates of construction for each, but roughly, Monticello I was built during 1768–1773 and Monticello II during 1794–1808. The only surviving parts of Monticello I were

Left: Monticello and pond, 2003 *Left, inset:* Portrait of Jefferson, c. 1791

those incorporated into its much larger successor, and most of what we know of it comes from Jefferson's surviving sketches, elevations, floor plans, and notes.

The beautifully restored house that greets visitors to Monticello today—which can be seen on the reverse of the nickel coin, from the vantage point of its western elevation—is only the final manifestation of Jefferson's continually evolving vision for his principal home. He produced the initial designs for Monticello I as a twenty-six-year-old bachelor planter and lawyer in 1768; Monticello II is generally considered to have been completed by 1809, the year he retired from two terms as the third president of the United States. And yet, work on the porticos was still going on in 1823, when Jefferson reached the age of eighty.

But both Monticellos reflected Jefferson's complex, restless personality; they were both continual works in progress. In keeping with his self-expressed passion for "building up and tearing down," Jefferson revised the interior and exterior designs again and again, adapting to the changing circumstances of his life and to the architectural influences—good and bad—that he encountered in his reading and in his travels in America and Europe.

Jefferson's desire for such a country home was not just a matter of class and upbringing. Jefferson certainly relished aspects of urban living—such as good food, wine, and the company of witty and creative people—but he held a lifelong conviction that the best life was agricultural and rural. This view echoed back to the farmer-senators of the Roman Republic and to Palladio's clients in Renaissance Italy. As Jefferson put it in *Notes on the State of Virginia*, "Those who labor in the earth are the chosen people of God, if ever He had a chosen people, whose breasts He has made [H]is peculiar deposit for substantial and genuine virtue." His attitude toward cities is summed up in an 1800 letter to the eminent physician Benjamin Rush: "I view great cities as pestilential to the morals, the health and the liberties of man. True, they nourish some of the elegant arts; but the useful ones can thrive elsewhere; and less perfection in the others, with more health, virtue and freedom, would be my choice."

MONTICELLO I

First, the setting: Monticello's site is a hilltop around 850 feet above sea level, and it was a place Jefferson knew from an early age. "I have heard my father say that when quite a boy the top of this mountain was his favorite retreat . . . and that the indescribable delight he here enjoyed so attached him to this spot, that he determined when he arrived at manhood he would here build his family mansion." Peter Jefferson didn't live to fulfill that ambition, but his son would make the site the foundation of one of America's greatest private residences.

How Monticello—"little mountain" in Italian—got its name isn't known exactly; the first use of the name appears in 1767, when Jefferson noted in his *Garden Books*—in which he kept meticulous records of his plantings—that he'd "inoculated common cherry buds into stocks of large kind at Monticello." There's evidence in his writings that he originally planned to call his home the Hermitage. Why he changed his mind, however, isn't known.

The site was an unusual choice for a family mansion. Monticello would not only be a residence, but also the focal point of a working plantation. (Monticello II would ultimately be home to more than 200 people—most of them slaves.) Most planters preferred their houses close to a river or road to better transport tobacco and other produce to market. What's more, building at such a high elevation would mean an uphill trip for visitors, tradesmen, and so on, not to mention the fact that it was hard to sink wells for water on a hilltop.

Above: The east façade and portico of Monticello, c. 1986 *Flap, front:* Aerial view of Monticello from the southwest *Flap, back:* The north façade of Monticello, c. 1986

For Jefferson, in this case, aesthetics trumped practicality. The house that Jefferson envisioned would take in a glorious view of the surrounding countryside, in keeping, perhaps, with Palladio's dictum that country houses should be built in "elevated and agreeable places." But, significantly, the house would face westward, toward the wild lands his father had surveyed—and where, Jefferson was already convinced, the future of America lay.

And the house that young Jefferson was visualizing would differ greatly from the mansions of his peers among the Virginia aristocracy, who still favored the Georgian style in vogue across the Atlantic in England. While the evidence is inconclusive, Jefferson may have been partly inspired by Robert Morris (1703–1754), one of Palladio's English interpreters. Morris was the author of a popular "pattern book," *Select Architecture*, with engraved plates of plans of representative houses. At the time, architecture was not the established profession it is today. It wouldn't be until 1865—nearly forty years after Jefferson's death—that a formal school of architecture was established in the United States, at the Massachusetts Institute of Technology. In eighteenth-century Britain and America, a gentleman with the means to build a substantial home would usually pick an appealing design from a pattern book and turn it over to a "housewright"—the chief contractor, essentially—to implement.

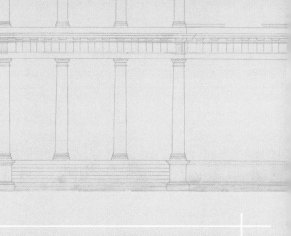

But Jefferson was far too individualistic to simply toss a plan at his housewright and tell him to get on with it. And it may also be the case that the 1770 fire that destroyed Jefferson's boyhood home, Shadwell,

Above: Jefferson's freehand drawing of Monticello's elevation, c. 1769-1770 *Background:* Jefferson's tracing of Pattern 3 from Robert Morris's book, *Select Architecture*

took his architectural books with it, forcing him to rely, at least in part, on his own imagination.

From about 1768 to 1771, Jefferson produced about twenty-five architectural drawings (or at least these are all that survive into the present) for Monticello I. To do so, Jefferson had to educate himself as a draftsman, probably using the tools—ruler and compass—that his father employed as a land surveyor.

Architectural historians consider Jefferson an "indifferent" draftsman, and he wasn't particularly gifted when it came to freehand drawing, either. But Jefferson knew what he wanted in a building, and he possessed the ability to communicate it—often in minute detail. His ongoing plans for Monticello and other buildings often included dimensions that were so mathematically precise that he had the measurements down to several decimal points.

This reflected another dimension of his personality; in modern terms, Jefferson was obsessive-compulsive. From youth until old age he obsessively recorded in writing everything from crop yields to the daily weather to the contents of his library, wine cellar, and everything in between. In architectural terms, though, the precision of Jefferson's plans likely frustrated the craftsmen and workers who had to turn his elevations and floor plans into reality. In the words of architectural historian Jack McLaughlin, such plans were "[An] absurdity in the building trades where carpenters and laborers are often lucky if they can keep to the inch rather than the ten-thousandth of an inch."

And by 1770, once the hilltop had been cleared and leveled, the carpenters and laborers were hard at work—digging the foundations, making bricks (Jefferson calculated that 310,000 would be needed), and cutting and milling timber for the woodwork.

For the design of Monticello I, Jefferson settled on a two-story central block, with a pedimented gable roof, flanked by one-story, hipped-roof wings to house service structures—pure Palladianism. And in keeping with that style, the central decorative element was a pedimented entrance portico—a two-story portico, in fact, with Doric columns on the first story and Ionic on the second. A man of Jefferson's social standing might have planned to decorate the pediment with his family's coat of arms, but unlike many of his fellow Virginian aristocrats, Jefferson wasn't particularly interested in genealogy. He specified a *lunette* (half-moon) window instead.

Opposite: Aerial view of Monticello's L-shaped terrace-topped wings *Enclosures:* Jefferson's drawings for Monticello: studies for the dependencies; mountaintop-layout plan showing the Lawn and a roundabout; cellar floor plan *Right, top:* Brickwork detail and cornice of Monticello's west façade, c. 1986 *Right, bottom:* The south service wing, or dependency, c. 1986

Because the house was to be the center of a working plantation, it required all manner of service structures, or what Jefferson called "dependencies": stables, storerooms, kitchens, workshops, smokehouses, icehouses, etc. Usually these dependencies took the form of freestanding outbuildings. At Monticello, however, Jefferson planned to integrate them into the main structure in the form of two L-shaped, semi-subterranean, terrace-topped wings, each terminating in a two-story pavilion.

Approaching the house's entrance portico, the service wings would be largely invisible, but the house's hilltop setting allowed the dependencies to have doors and windows on the rearward, downward slope. The ingenious scheme is a prime example of Jefferson's flair for combining the aesthetic and the practical—it would minimize residents' and visitors' exposure to the smell and smoke of cooking and the bustle and noise of a busy plantation community. (This part of the plan would not be fully realized, however, until the completion of Monticello II decades later.)

The first part of Monticello I to rise from Jefferson's hilltop was a modest brick cottage. Its eventual function was to be one of the aforementioned pavilions, but when Jefferson moved into it in late 1770, it served as his bachelor quarters while work on the main house went on. Shortly after settling in, Jefferson wrote that "[The cottage,] like the cobbler's, serves me for parlor, for kitchen and hall, I may add for bed chamber and study, too…. I have hope, however, of getting more elbow room this summer."

The bachelor's quarters became the Honeymoon Cottage in January 1772 when Jefferson brought home his new bride, the vivacious Martha Wayles Skelton, better known as Patty. They arrived in a blizzard and found a cold fireplace, but there was a bottle of wine and "song, merriment, and laughter." It was a happy start to what by all accounts was a happy marriage. It produced six children, though only two of them—Martha (born in 1772) and Maria (born in 1778)—lived to adulthood.

It's possible that Patty Jefferson influenced the ongoing construction project that was Monticello I. As originally planned, the main house was fairly modest in its interior proportions—just four rooms on the main floor (entrance hall, parlor, dining room, master bedroom), and another room on the second floor. But, as all parents learn, when children arrive, more space is needed, and additional rooms were added to the wings. The additions were semi-octagons. (The octagon fascinated Jefferson, and he incorporated it, in various forms, into many of his designs.)

The house was habitable, if far from being complete in all its details, by around 1773. But over the next few years Jefferson would be called away from Monticello for longer and longer periods of time as Virginia and the other colonies grew restive under British rule. In 1774, Jefferson wrote "A Summary View of the Rights of British North America." The work was intended only as a set of arguments and instructions for Virginia's delegation to the First Continental Congress, but it was reprinted throughout the colonies, and it won Jefferson a reputation as a persuasive advocate for the Patriot cause. Arriving in Philadelphia for the Second Continental Congress in the summer of 1776, he became the principal writer of the Declaration of Independence.

In 1779—a year after the completion of Monticello's brickwork—Jefferson became governor of Virginia, which was now a state following the 1776 Declaration of Independence. The military focus of the War for Independence had shifted to the South, and in May 1781, Jefferson and his family had to flee Monticello just minutes before British and Loyalist cavalry charged up the hill. The soldiers occupied the house for the better part of the day, but did no damage other than raiding the wine cellar.

The fighting ended with the Patriot victory at Yorktown later that year, but Jefferson wouldn't be able to enjoy the coming of peace and independence. Worn out by illness and childbearing, Patty Jefferson died in September 1782. Jefferson was devastated, describing himself as "a blank which I had not the spirits to fill up." He vowed not to remarry and he never did. Distracted by grief, he largely stopped work on the final refinements to Monticello.

Above: Engraving of Patty Jefferson *Opposite:* Final first-floor plan of Monticello I showing octagonal rooms added to each wing, c. 1771

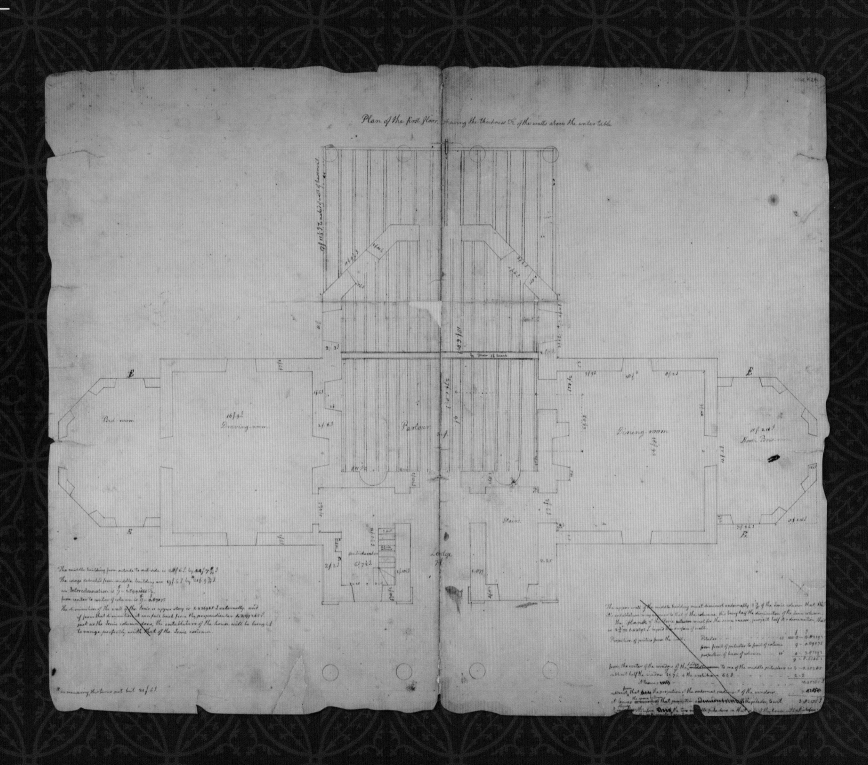

Plan of the first floor, shewing the thickness &c. of the walls above the water table

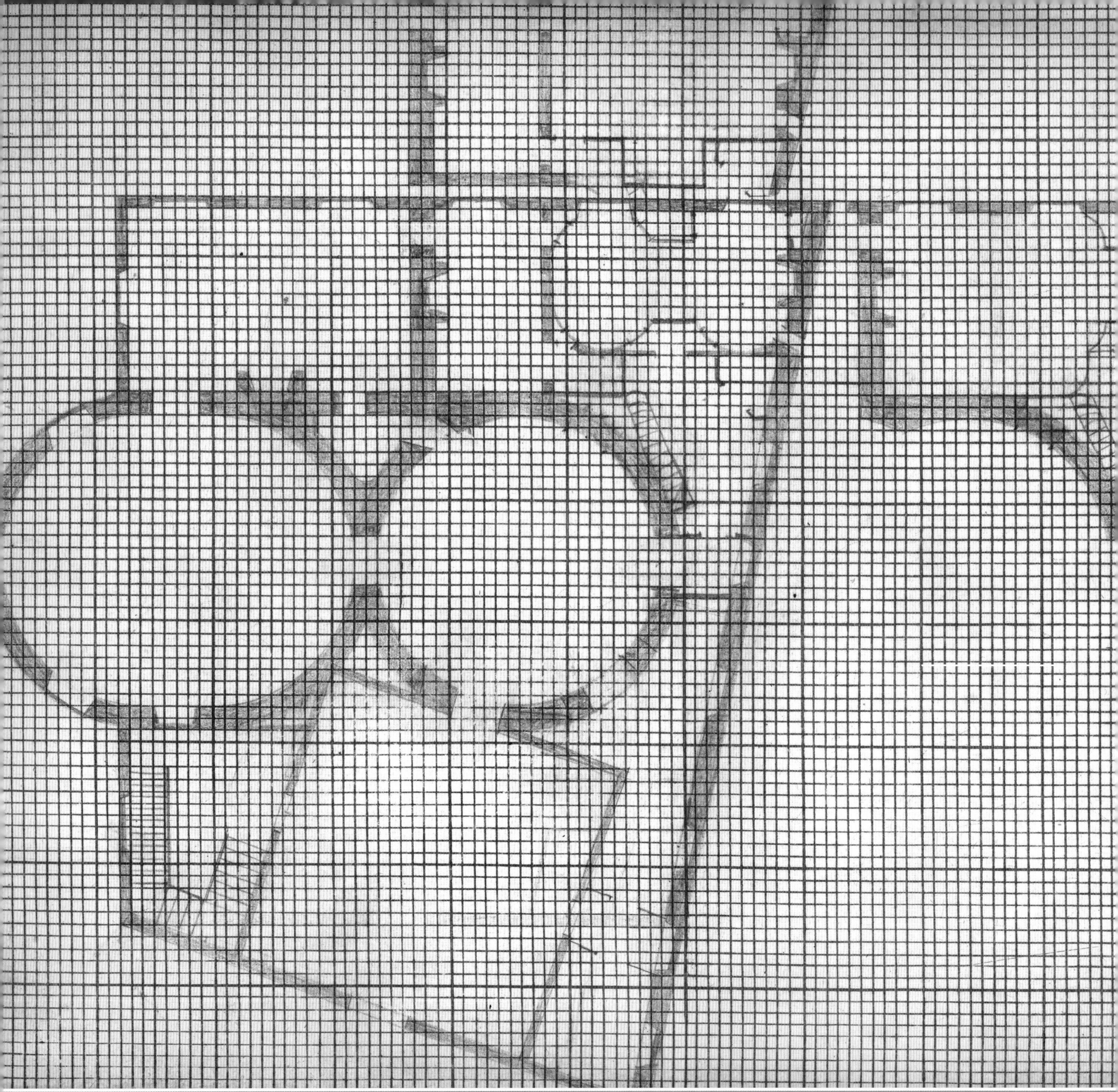

Jefferson in Paris—and Elsewhere

Now a widower on the cusp of middle age, Jefferson had never traveled farther away from Virginia than New York City, and then only briefly. That changed in the spring of 1784, when Congress appointed him as Minister to France. Jefferson's diplomatic duties would keep him in Europe for the better part of five years. Paris was his base, but between official missions and personal travel, he visited England, Germany, Holland, and Italy—although to his regret he never went to Rome to visit the ruins that inspired Palladio, the author of his architectural "bible." With his architectural eye honed by more than a decade of work on Monticello and his reading on the subject, he closely examined the notable buildings he encountered in Europe—ancient and contemporary—and their influence would be visible in his later designs.

In August 1784, Jefferson and his daughter Martha (later joined by Maria) settled into a rented residence, the Hotel de Langeac, on the Champs-Élysées. (In this context, hotel means town house.) "I am savage enough to prefer the woods, the wilds, and the independence of Monticello, to all the brilliant pleasure of this gay capital," he wrote in 1785. But he clearly found a lot to like in the City of Light. There were the paintings in the Louvre to contemplate, bookstores full of rare volumes to browse, and witty conversations in the salons where the intellectual elite gathered.

Jefferson arrived in Paris at a time when the city was in the midst of a building boom—"every day [the city is] enlarging and beautifying," in his words. One of the new buildings was another town house, the Hotel de Salm, which was still under construction when Jefferson arrived. He liked to rent a chair in the Tuileries to watch its progress, and told a friend he was "violently smitten" with it. He was smitten enough to draw inspiration for some significant elements of what would become Monticello II. Like other fashionable Parisian town houses, the Hotel de Salm gave the impression of being one story from the outside—so Jefferson did away with the plan for a two-story portico for Monticello II. To maximize interior space, Parisian town houses eschewed a "grand staircase" in favor of smaller, steeper staircases—so Jefferson adopted the same approach for Monticello II.

Another building that caught Jefferson's eye was the Halle aux Bleds—the city's public grain market—which was topped by a windowed dome. Jefferson was captivated both by the way the dome let light into the market's vast interior and by its construction. Rather than the masonry traditionally used in domes, it was wood-framed—a modern adaptation of a Renaissance technique sometimes called "sticks and chips." To Jefferson, it seemed a method ideally suited for building in America, where there was a lot of wood and not much cut stone—or many skilled stonemasons. This was probably the genesis, in Jefferson's mind, of what would literally be Monticello II's crowning feature.

Something else caught Jefferson's eye when he visited the Halle aux Bleds with the American painter John Trumbull in August 1786. Trumbull introduced Jefferson to Maria Cosway, the twenty-seven-year-old wife of English artist Richard Cosway, and an accomplished artist and musician herself. Jefferson and Maria formed a close friendship; whether the relationship progressed beyond that isn't known for sure.

Opposite: Plan of Hotel de Langeac in Paris, c. 1785 *Above:* Engraving of Maria Cosway *Background:* Jefferson's drawing for Monticello's main stairs, c. 1771

By pure coincidence, Jefferson left Paris in September 1789, just a couple of months after the French Revolution began. He brought back crate upon crate of furniture, artwork and books, a taste for gourmet food and vintage wines, a renewed spirit, and new ideas for the next edition of what he described as "my architectural essay"—Monticello.

But before he could begin to expand his home, politics again intervened.

MONTICELLO II

In 1790, Jefferson became the nation's first secretary of state in President George Washington's cabinet. There he butted political heads with Alexander Hamilton, the secretary of the treasury, over which direction the new United States of America should take. Jefferson wanted an agrarian society with limited central government; Hamilton wanted a more commercial nation with strong federal authority over the states. This split led to the development of political parties, with Hamilton's supporters lining up under the Federalist banner, while Jefferson and his fellow Virginians formed the Democratic-Republican Party. There was wrangling over foreign policy, too, with the Federalists largely hostile to the revolutionary government in France, while Jefferson and his allies favored maintaining ties with the country that, after all, had helped America achieve independence.

After three years of turmoil in the cabinet, Jefferson decided he wanted out. He missed, as he put it, "my family, my farm, and my books," and furthermore, "I have my house to build." In 1793 he resigned, and for the next few years he rarely left Monticello.

It's significant that Jefferson used the verb "build," because he was indeed planning what was essentially an entirely new structure instead of just expanding and modifying the old one. Monticello I disappeared into Monticello II; the latter, which ultimately enclosed about 11,000 square feet of living space, was more than twice the size of the former.

Much of Monticello I, including the portico and the roof, had to be demolished to implement Jefferson's new plans. This was done between 1794 and 1796, when construction began in earnest. Jefferson was now keeping a "remodelling notebook" in his usual meticulous way—jotting down, for example, which of the classical orders he would use as the decorative scheme in each room.

As during the construction of Monticello I, skilled workers did the more technical jobs on Monticello II, assisted by slaves. And it should be noted that the slaves provided more than muscle power. Over time, many of the white workers (who worked for wages) at Monticello II departed after imparting their skills, like bricklaying or blacksmithing, to Jefferson's slaves. Eventually, Jefferson could draw on

Above: Monticello's reflection on the pond, c. 1984 *Enclosures:* Jefferson's plans for Monticello, c. 1771: proposed five-story observation tower; final elevation for Monticello I

Jefferson and Slavery

The use of slave labor on Monticello—and Jefferson's other projects—brings up the great paradox of his life for contemporary Americans; it's hard to process that the man responsible for those ringing words: "We hold these truths to be self-evident, that all men are created equal," and who believed passionately in individual liberty, *owned* other human beings. The eighteenth-century English writer Samuel Johnson summed it up perfectly when he said, in reference to Jefferson and his fellow American revolutionaries, "How is it that we hear the loudest yelps for liberty among the drivers of Negroes?"

Jefferson opposed slavery in principle, but he was completely dependent on the system financially. The truth is that Jefferson was terrible with money. He raised wheat as a cash crop at Monticello and built a foundry for making nails for sale commercially, but the income never covered the bills. And although Jefferson cultivated an image of "republican simplicity," his taste for the finer things—and, of course, the grand project of Monticello—led him to overspend wildly, driving him deeper and deeper into debt. Jefferson's human property was his major asset, one he couldn't give up if he hoped to maintain his lifestyle and indulge his many interests.

Then there's the matter of Sally Hemings, or Hemmings, as the surname is alternatively spelled. Born in 1773, she was a slave of Jefferson's father-in-law, John Wayles, and Patty Jefferson inherited her upon his death. (Some historians believe that John Wayles was Sally Hemings's father—making her and Patty half sisters.) In 1802, some of Jefferson's political enemies published accusations that Sally Hemings was Jefferson's longtime "mistress" and that he'd fathered several of her children. (The craftsman John Hemings was her brother: see p. 32.)

The controversy has divided historians ever since. Modern DNA testing has shown a genetic link between Jefferson and Hemings descendants, but that doesn't prove Jefferson himself was the father of any of Sally Hemings's children. If it is true that Jefferson had such a relationship—beyond the moral implications of a relationship in which one party is the other's property—it was an act of hypocrisy, coming from a man who once wrote "[T]he amalgamation of whites with blacks produces a degradation to which no lover of his country, no lover of excellence in the human character, can innocently consent." Jefferson's reservations about slavery didn't extend to any idea of the equality of the races, but in this he was no different from most white men of his time.

Right: Page from Jefferson's *Farm Book* listing Sally Hemings among his slaves (middle column)

a team of talented slave artisans to do much of the more demanding work on his upgraded mountaintop home.

The most prominent of these slave artisans was John Hemings (c. 1776–1830), who would play an important part in creating Monticello II. (There was much history between the Jeffersons and the Hemings; see p.31) As an apprentice to the white craftsmen Jefferson initially hired, John Hemings became a skilled joiner and furniture maker, responsible for much of the house's interior work. He also built a Campeachy chair—a kind of recliner—that eased Jefferson's rheumatic back.

The de facto team leader for all the workers on Monticello II—whether slave or free—was Irish-born James Dinsmore (c. 1771–1830), whom Jefferson described as "a house joiner . . . of the very first order," and who arrived at Monticello in 1798; he stayed for eleven years and, with John Hemings assisting, did much of the fine interior woodworking, such as moldings and cornices.

Dinsmore was also responsible for Monticello II's iconic feature, the Dome. Other (non-slave) artisans included another Irish-born joiner, John Neilson (who liked to borrow Jefferson's copy of Palladio's *The Four Books*); the stonemason Hugh Chisholm; the framer John Perry; and Richard Barry, who painted the interior—a two-year project.

Jefferson was fortunate to have a cadre of craftsmen that he could trust, because once again he was in the political arena and usually had to oversee construction from afar—which, given his compulsive personality, would have certainly made him nervous if he didn't think his house was in good hands.

Jefferson was elected vice president in 1796 under John Adams; four years later, he entered the "President's House" in the capital, after a hotly contested race. His first term was fairly successful, highlighted by the purchase of the Louisiana Territory, which doubled the size of the United States for pennies an

Above: Final west elevation of Monticello II by American architect Robert Mills, 1803 *Flap:* Decorative outchamber of Monticello with Ionic portico and dome, c. 1778 *Opposite:* Oil painting of Monticello, nineteenth century

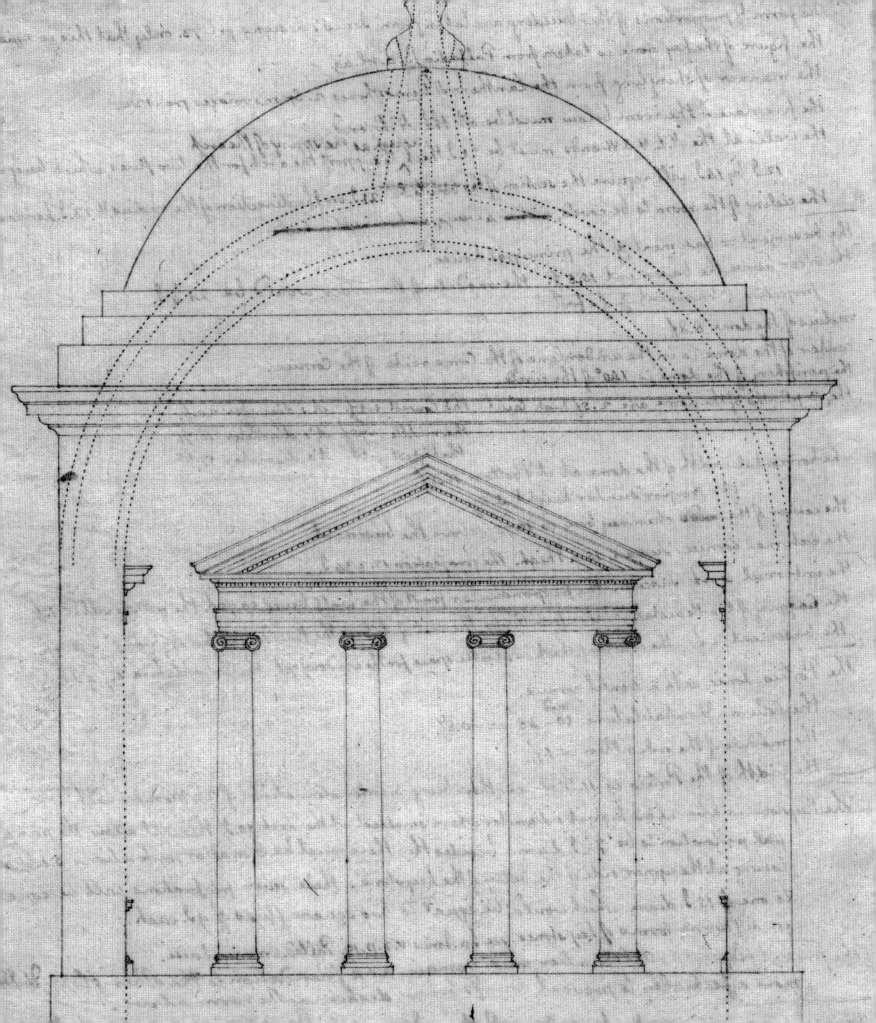

Jefferson the Inventor

Jefferson was the prototypical American "gadget freak," obsessed with finding devices to do things more efficiently—or, if need be, inventing such devices himself. Jefferson's inventions ranged from a plow with an iron moldboard to better plow hillsides to a machine for making pasta, which he'd developed a taste for in Europe. He wrote the Declaration of Independence on a portable desk of his own design (a replica of which can be seen at the restored Monticello), and as secretary of state he developed a simple but secure "wheel cipher" for encoding and decoding diplomatic correspondence. Besides his own inventions, Jefferson adapted or improved upon mechanical innovations that he came across in his reading, his travels, or his contact with like-minded friends.

THE POLYGRAPH

Jefferson's cabinet, or study, included a polygraph. Not a lie detector, but an early form of a copying machine, which combined two pens in a framework: writing with one pen made an exact copy on a second sheet, allowing Jefferson to keep a letter-perfect record of all his correspondence. The polygraph is an example of a device Jefferson didn't invent, but one he championed. It was the brainchild of an Englishman, John Isaac Hawkins. Jefferson likely learned of the polygraph from his friend, the artist Charles Willson Peale, who had acquired the American rights to the device. Jefferson got his hands on one in 1804, proclaimed it "the finest invention of the present age," and used various models for the rest of his life. (Prior to acquiring the polygraph, Jefferson copied his letters using a "copy press," which simply transferred the damp ink impression from the original to a blank sheet and left much to be desired regarding elegance and accuracy.)

SPHERICAL SUNDIAL

Sometime between 1809 and 1816, Jefferson—inspired by some ideas from Benjamin Latrobe, designer of the U.S. Capitol—designed and built a sundial for Monticello's North Terrace. Sundials had been around for thousands of years, of course, but Jefferson's was different—it was spherical. As he wrote to Latrobe: "It occurred then [to me] that [a] globe might be made to perform the functions of a dial. I ascertained on it two poles, delineated its equator and tropics, described meridians at every 15 degrees from tropic to tropic, and shorter portions of meridian intermediately for the half hours, quarter hours, and every 5 minutes . . . Perhaps indeed this may be no novelty. It is one however to me."

A Tour of Mr. Jefferson's House

When Jefferson returned in 1809, the house in which the sixty-six-year-old ex-president would spend his remaining twenty-seven years of life now stretched more than 110 feet in length across the hilltop. Visitors ascended what one described as a "steep, savage hill" via a curved drive Jefferson called a "roundabout."

The main entrance to the house for visitors was the Northeast Portico, which opened into the Entrance Hall, a reception room about twenty-eight by twenty-four feet with a ceiling extending over eighteen feet to the mezzanine above. The hall served as a filtering space—guests were greeted here, and then admitted to the public and private rooms beyond depending on their status and degree of intimacy with Jefferson and his family members. And Jefferson always had plenty of guests—some invited, some not. His daughter Maria once complained to him about the "concourse of strangers" constantly coming up the drive.

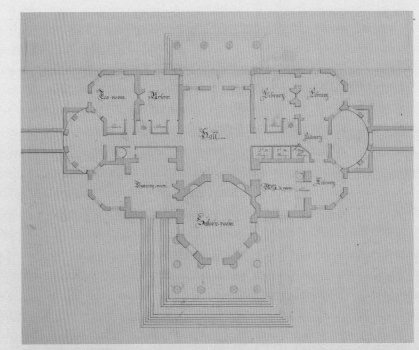

The Entrance Hall became popularly known as the Indian Hall because Jefferson decorated its whitewashed walls with Native American artifacts and relics. George Ticknor, a young Bostonian who visited Monticello in 1815 and left a priceless account of the experience, described the décor: "On one side hangs the head and horns of an elk, a deer, and a buffalo. Another is covered with curiosities, which Lewis and Clarke [sic] found in their wild and perilous expedition. On the third, among many other striking matters, is the head of a mammoth. . . ." This last item was actually the fossilized jawbone of a mastodon, fruit of an archaeological dig in Kentucky that Jefferson had helped organize. At the suggestion of painter Gilbert Stuart, the floor covering was painted "grass green" to emphasize the "natural" theme.

The Entrance Hall was flanked by two rooms: the South Square Room and the North Square Room. The former was a kind of family sitting room (it also apparently housed some of the overflow from Jefferson's library); the latter was a guest room for distinguished visitors.

Beyond the Entrance Hall was the semi-octagonal Parlor, which had the same functions as a living room in a modern house. Roughly the same dimensions as the Entrance Hall, it featured a parquet floor of cherry and beech—one of the first parquet floors in the United States. Here family and guests could talk, play cards, and listen to music provided by Jefferson himself on his beloved violin, perhaps accompanied by his daughter Martha on a harpsichord Jefferson had commissioned from one of London's finest instrument makers. The rear of the Parlor opened to the Southwest

Right, top: Floor plan of Monticello by American architect Robert Mills, c. 1803 *Right, bottom:* Native American artifacts hanging in Monticello's Entrance Hall

Alcove beds were a typical space-saving Jefferson touch—why waste floor space that could be given over to other, waking activities?

Next, the Book Room, or Library, housed Jefferson's ever-expanding collection—which would eventually reach almost 6,000 volumes. Jefferson was choosy about whom he admitted to the Book Room. One curious visitor sniffed that "he keeps it constantly locked, and I have been much disappointed by trying to get in."

Rounding out Jefferson's personal space was the Southeast Piazza, or Greenhouse, where he experimented with growing various species of plants and relaxed by doing metalwork on his workbench. On either side of the Southeast Piazza was a small porch (Jefferson called them "porticles") where he could read or write when the weather was fine. The porticles also gave Jefferson a measure of privacy, as their placement prevented nosy guests from a direct view of his quarters.

To the right of the Parlor, facing west, was the Dining Room, which connected to the smaller, more intimate Tea Room; for large dinners and other gatherings, the two rooms could function as one entertaining space.

Returning to the interior, the North Wing of the house included another piazza—the North Piazza—and the North Octagonal Room; like the North Square Room, it served as a guest bedroom or sitting room. Also, like the North Square Room (and Jefferson's own Bedchamber), the bed was recessed into an alcove.

From the piazzas at either end, one could walk out on the terraces that roofed the dependencies, and to the two-story Pavilions. Distanced as they were from the main house, the Pavilions were quiet and private.

The house's second and third floors, accessed by the narrow staircases that some guests complained about, were family bedrooms and various passageways and storage areas. The third floor was also the site of the room enclosed by the Dome—known, naturally, as the Dome Room—which was topped by a four-and-a-half-foot oculus (dome window) special-ordered from a Boston glazier in 1805. Oddly enough, no one is sure what purpose the Dome Room, beautiful as it was, served. It may have been used as a playroom by Jefferson's grandchildren or just as a storage space.

By the standards of its times, Monticello II was a more comfortable place to live than most "grand" American homes. Jefferson certainly took great pains with lighting and ventilation, making use of triple-hung sash windows and skylights—twelve of them, in addition to the oculus in the Dome Room—that could be opened to let in fresh air. The skylights were especially necessary on the third floor; in order to preserve the outward appearance of a one-story house, Parisian-style, Monticello II's main floor windows extended up a bit beyond floor level on the second floor, but the third-floor rooms were windowless.

Portico, sometimes called the Garden Portico, overlooking the West Lawn. The view of the house from the West Lawn, with the Dome fully visible, is the image of Monticello most people are familiar with—it's the one that appears on the nickel. And it should be noted that officially, there was no "back" or "front" at Monticello; Jefferson tended to refer to the porticos and their façades as the "East Front" and the "West Front."

Jefferson's personal quarters—into which the intensely private man rarely invited guests—comprised most of the house's South Wing. Jefferson's Bedchamber, off the Parlor, featured an eighteen-and-a-half-foot ceiling inset with a skylight. Beyond the Bedchamber was Jefferson's Study—or, as he called it in the French fashion, his Cabinet. The two rooms were connected by an alcove in which Jefferson had his bed, with storage space above reached by a ladder.

Comfort was limited by the technology of the time, of course. Heat came from eight fireplaces and two wood-burning stoves, light from candles and whale-oil lamps. For answering calls of nature, there were three small "air-closets"—toilets—inside the house, one in Jefferson's private quarters. Arrangements like this were unusual then, but they did not constitute indoor plumbing. Later accounts that the air-closets emptied into some kind of cesspool have been proved false; probably, the air-closets just had the usual chamber pot under the seat.

Architectural historian Spiro Kostof describes Monticello's legacy:

> Fixed to the land with its domed core but acknowledging with its outstretched wings the open-ended expanse, and filled with gadgets of all kinds, Monticello was like the primordial American home—seeking stability but also freedom, respectful of European tradition but insistent on comfort and effort-saving devices, both conventional and one of a kind.

MONTICELLO AFTER JEFFERSON

In 1787, Jefferson wrote from Europe: "I am as happy no where else and in no other society, and all my wishes end, where I hope my days will end, at Monticello. Too many scenes of happiness mingle themselves with all the recollections of my native woods and fields, to suffer them to be supplanted in my affection by any other." He achieved his goal of ending his days at Monticello, and he did indeed experience many scenes of happiness there.

Jefferson's long retirement was marred by his continual, and worsening, money troubles. To keep his creditors at bay, he sold his precious library to the federal government to restock the original Library of Congress. (The LOC lost its original collection when the British burned Washington, D.C.) In the final year of his life, the state government of Virginia approved a special lottery to keep Jefferson out of bankruptcy, but the scheme fell apart. By then, Monticello was in a shabby state, inside and out.

Jefferson's death on July 4, 1826—the fiftieth anniversary of the Declaration of Independence—left debts of more than $100,000 for his heirs to settle. A year later, the house's furnishings and much of his other property, including his slaves, were sold, the proceeds going to his creditors. (Jefferson only freed five of his slaves in his will: they included John Hemings and two of Sally Hemings's children—but not Sally Hemings herself.)

Opposite: Greenhouse at Monticello *Right, top:* Dome Room at Monticello; room is generally closed to public viewing *Right, bottom:* Jefferson's Bedchamber with the alcove bed, looking through to the Cabinet room, c. 1986

Jefferson had desperately hoped Monticello would stay in his family but, in 1831, the house and 550 acres of land was sold for $4,500 to a man who attempted to use the property to raise silkworms. He failed and sold Monticello a few years later.

In 1834, the house came into the possession of Uriah P. Levy (1792–1862). The first Jew to serve a full career in the U.S. Navy, Levy greatly admired Jefferson's stance on religious freedom, and he planned to restore Monticello as a monument. Levy failed to fully achieve his goal before he died in 1862, by which time the Civil War had broken out, and the Confederate government seized Monticello and sold it yet again. After the war, Levy's nephew—the aptly named Jefferson Levy—waged a long, complicated legal battle to win back control of the property. He succeeded in 1879.

In 1923, a nonprofit organization, the Thomas Jefferson Foundation, acquired Monticello. Restoration had begun under Jefferson Levy's ownership and continued under the foundation; among those who worked on the project was Fiske Kimball (1888–1955), the scholar who first championed Jefferson as a great architect. As architectural historian Hugh Howard points out, though, the restored Monticello "as beautiful as it is, is a painstaking reconstruction of a place with more polish than Jefferson could ever apply."

With the possible exception of Frank Lloyd Wright's Fallingwater (built 1934–1937), Monticello is the most celebrated private home in America—indeed, it's the only private residence in the United States to be named a World Heritage Site by the United Nations Educational, Scientific, and Cultural Organization (UNESCO), an honor it received in 1987. (The honor was shared with another of Jefferson's great designs, the "Academical Village" at the University of Virginia.)

For all the art and artifice that went into the building of Monticello I and II, it was the American landscape surrounding the house that most soothed Jefferson's soul and inspired his spirit. As he wrote in 1786:

And our own dear Monticello, where has nature spread so rich a mantel under the eye? mountains, forests, rocks, rivers. With what majesty do we there ride above the storms! How sublime to look down into the workhouse of nature, to see her clouds, hail, snow, rain, thunder, all fabricated at our feet! And the glorious Sun, when rising as if out of a distant water, just gilding the tops of the mountains, and giving life to all nature!

Right: Twilight at Monticello, 2004

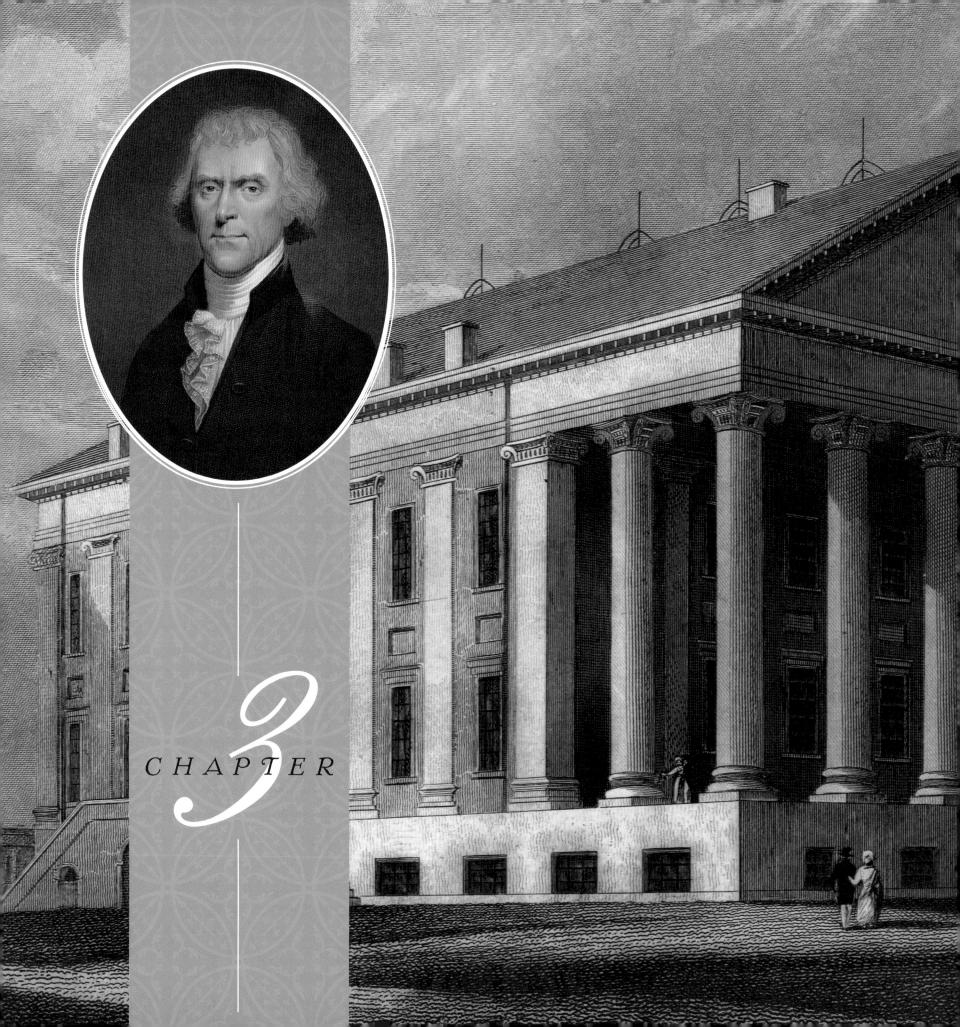

CHAPTER 3

Jamestown to Williamsburg to Richmond

Virginia's first capital was Jamestown—the first successful English colony in what would become the United States, settled in 1607. It was here, in 1619, that America's first elected legislature—the House of Burgesses—met. (That year also marked the beginning of a more pernicious legacy with the arrival of the first African slaves in the colony.) The timber buildings of Jamestown, however, had a tendency to burn down. After fire claimed the fourth version of the Burgesses's meeting place in 1698, the capital relocated to Middle Plantation, soon renamed Williamsburg after King William III of England (reigned 1689–1702). Reportedly, the move came at the urging of students and faculty at Jefferson's alma mater, the College of William and Mary—the climate, it was thought, would be more congenial.

The legislature and the colony's General Court met in the college's Wren Building until a new Capitol building was completed in 1705. Forty-two years later, it too burned down. The legislature and the Court went back to the Wren Building once again, until a new Capitol opened for business in 1753. This Georgian structure was the one that Jefferson came to know as a young student, lawyer, and legislator, and in the run-up to the Revolution it saw dramatic scenes like Patrick Henry's "Give me liberty or give me death!" speech. (The reconstructed version of this building is now the centerpiece of Colonial Williamsburg; the massive restoration began in the late 1920s and was financed by the Rockefeller family.)

As noted, Jefferson didn't have much love for the buildings of Williamsburg, although he did single out the 1753 Capitol—which was actually two structures with a connecting arcade—for faint praise, writing in his *Notes on the State of Virginia* that:

> [It was] a light and airy structure, with a portico in front of two orders, the lower of which, being Doric, is tolerably just in its proportions and ornaments, save only that the intercolumniations are too large. The upper is Ionic, much too small for that on which it is mounted, its ornaments not proper to the order, nor proportioned within themselves. It is crowned with a pediment, which is too high for its span. Yet on the whole, it is the most pleasing piece of architecture we have.

Even before the Revolutionary War broke out, some prominent Virginians argued that the seat of government should move out of Williamsburg—a proposal that Jefferson

wholeheartedly supported. While situated on a higher elevation than Jamestown, Williamsburg was still within the low-lying Tidewater region, where the heat and humidity in the summer bred insects and consequent diseases. On a more philosophical level, Jefferson—who always had his eyes fixed firmly on the western frontier rather than the coastal littoral—wanted the capital located farther inland. Relocation became a matter of urgency when fighting with Britain broke out in the spring of 1775: Williamsburg, not far from the Atlantic, was clearly vulnerable to attack.

In 1776, the year of independence, Jefferson submitted a "Bill for the Removal of the Seat of Government of Virginia" to the legislature. The bill languished until 1779, when Jefferson became governor and managed to ram the bill through in a matter of days. It moved the capital to Richmond, a town on the James River about fifty-five miles west of Williamsburg. The legislature—now known as the Virginia General Assembly—met there for the first time, in a former tobacco warehouse, in 1780.

Jefferson himself drew up the plat (the basic town plan) for Richmond, including sites for the various public buildings. And he was also clearly thinking about designs for the Capitol building itself—he'd envisioned a structure based on classical temples, using the Ionic order, in the mid-1770s, although these initial designs may have been intended as a new Capitol building for Williamsburg. But with the move to Richmond, Jefferson definitely had a site in mind for the new Capitol—Shockhoe Hill, overlooking the falls of the James River. Like Monticello, this structure would be placed on a high elevation.

Above: South façade of the reconstructed original Capitol in Williamsburg, Virginia

By 1785, the Virginia legislators were tired of debating and voting in a dingy and no doubt smelly old tobacco barn. This prompted the momentous letter from "Messrs. Buchanan and Hay" asking for Jefferson to procure a design for a Capitol building that would house "apartments . . . for the use of the legislative, executive, and judiciary . . . under one roof."

What's more, the Virginia government wanted the design immediately. But Jefferson believed the job was too important to be done in haste. He replied that he saw two options: "One was to leave to some architect to draw an external according to his fancy, in which way experience shews [*sic*] that about once in a thousand times a pleasing form is hit upon; the other was to take some model already applied and approved by the general suffrage [approval] of the world."

So Jefferson clearly wanted "some model" on which to base the Capitol building for his beloved Virginia. But what would that model be?

MONSIEUR CLÉRISSEAU AND THE MAISON CARRÉE

The man whom Jefferson described as an "able architect" was indeed a remarkable figure. Sixty-three years old when Jefferson first met with him in 1785, Charles-Louis Clérisseau (1721–1820) had spent the better part of two decades in Rome, producing paintings of the city's ancient ruins (he was a student of the artist Giovanni Paolo Panini) and serving as a cicerone—a kind of tour guide.

In the eighteenth century, no well-born young male Briton's education was complete without a "Grand Tour" of continental Europe following graduation from Oxford or Cambridge, and Rome was a major stop on the itinerary. Clérisseau introduced many of these young gentlemen, including a Scotsman with architectural ambitions named Robert Adam (1728–1792), to the surviving classical buildings of Rome and other destinations in Italy and southern France. Inspired by Clérisseau, Adam and his brothers James (1732–1794) and John (1721–1792) became the foremost exponents of the Neoclassical style of architecture in Britain (Robert especially). As Robert wrote in 1755, "I found out Clérisseau . . . in whom there is no guile, Yet there is the utmost knowledge of Architecture of perspective, & of Design and Colouring I ever Saw, or had any Conception of; he rais'd my ideas, He created emulation & fire in my breast. I wish'd above all things to learn in his manner. . . ."

Left: Elevation for the Maison Carrée from Andrea Palladio's *The Four Books*, which is strikingly similar to Jefferson's plan for the Capitol building

But while Robert Adam went on to become the foremost British vernacular architect of the late eighteenth century, Clérisseau's own architectural ambitions were largely frustrated until Jefferson walked into his Paris atelier. His one major commission—a country villa for Catherine the Great—had been rejected as unsuitable for the Russian climate. In the mid-1780s, Clérisseau was known mainly as a painter and "antiquarian."

But Jefferson and Clérisseau quickly found themselves kindred spirits in their mutual love of the grace and beauty of classical architecture: "The love I have for my art," Clérisseau would write to Jefferson, "is such that I cannot express to you how much I have been gratified to find [in you] a true lover of antiquity."

Jefferson already had definite ideas about what he wanted in a Capitol when he met Clérisseau: a purely classical design, maybe based on the Roman Temple of the Sun at Baalbek, in what is now Lebanon . . . or the Erechtheum, a Greek temple built around 400 BCE as part of the Acropolis in Athens . . . or perhaps the Maison

Carrée, a Roman temple built around 20 BCE in Nîmes in southern France. (The structure got its name from the French term *carré* for long, or rectangle.)

Jefferson only knew the Maison Carrée from its depiction by his beloved Palladio. But Clérisseau was intimately familiar with it, having studied it personally and included it in his book *Antiquités de la France*, an oversized tome that the American diplomat and the French antiquarian perused that day. And so it was decided: the Maison Carrée would be the template for Virginia's new Capitol.

Measuring roughly eighty-seven by fifty-four feet and raised aboveground on a pediment about nine-and-a-half feet in height, the Maison Carrée has pediment porticos (pronaos) on either end, each supported by six Corinthian columns. It was built under the patronage of the Roman statesman and military commander Marcus Vipsanius Agrippa (63–12 BCE)—who was also responsible for the construction of the Pantheon in Rome—and was dedicated to his sons. Jefferson had not yet seen the Maison Carrée, which is one of the best-preserved buildings of the Roman

Above: Painting of the Maison Carrée with the Amphitheatre and the Tour Magne at Nîmes, 1787

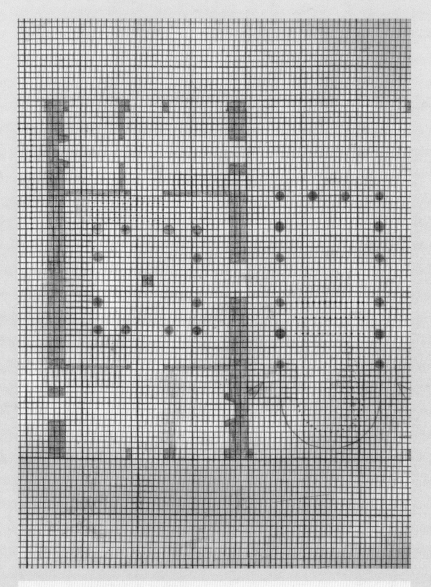

Empire. It served, at various times over the centuries, as a Christian church, a stable, a government facility, and a municipal archive. (It's been a museum since the 1820s; in our own time, an art gallery, the Carrée d'Art, was built nearby from a design by the British architect Sir Norman Foster.)

In March 1787, Jefferson finally viewed the temple with his own eyes on a tour of southern France; just as he had written that he was "violently smitten" by the Hotel de Salm in Paris, he would use the language of love to describe his reaction to the Maison Carrée, writing to a Parisian friend: "Here I am, Madam, gazing whole hours at the Maison quarree [*sic*], like a lover at his mistress" and declaring it "to be the most perfect and precious remain of antiquity in existence."

Paper to Plaster to Reality

By then the Jefferson/Clérisseau design for the Capitol was well advanced. And the plans themselves embodied an innovation. While browsing for yet more books, Jefferson had visited a shop in the city's Latin Quarter, where he encountered a curious sort of paper. The sheets were printed with a raised grid—ten squares to the inch. The paper was intended to help silk weavers keep to pattern, but Jefferson was quick to grasp its potential for building design; as he wrote, it "saves the necessity of using the rule and dividers in all rectangular draughts." At the time it was known as "coordinate paper"; today it's called graph paper.

As for the Capitol's design, the plan had to be adapted to the needs of the state government. As a temple, the Maison Carrée's interior was basically one large open space, but the Capitol would need to contain the two houses of the Assembly, a courtroom, and various offices. So the building would be a hybrid—a near-direct copy of a classical structure from the outside with a more conventional statehouse layout within. In keeping with Jefferson's love of light and airy spaces, though, the interior would include a spacious, skylit lobby separating the legislative and judicial spaces; it would also display a magnificent statue of George Washington by Jean-Antoine Houdon.

Just how much of the overall design was Clérisseau's and how much was Jefferson's is still a subject of debate. But, as with Monticello, Jefferson knew what he wanted—for example, he decided that the Capitol's columns would be Ionic, rather than the Corinthian order used in the Maison Carrée, although he may have bowed to Clérisseau's suggestion to deepen the Capitol's portico.

Coordinate Paper

European craftsman and designers had used "squared" or "coordinate" paper marked with precisely measured grids for centuries before Jefferson encountered the medium in Paris—around the time such paper began to be specially printed, instead of just having the lines drawn on plain paper by a draftsman. Fiske Kimball—a re-discoverer of Jefferson's architectural legacy—believed that Jefferson took to coordinate paper with enthusiasm because it enabled him "to employ a freer medium in spite of his deficiencies of technique." However, Jefferson continued to draw mostly in pen and ink, largely ignoring another innovation of the era—the lead (actually graphite) pencil.

Left: Plan for the Virginia Capitol on coordinate paper, 1785 *Enclosures:* Plans for the Virginia Capitol, 1785: side elevation of the Capitol showing a portico on one end of the building; Capitol plan on coordinate paper *Opposite:* Virginia Capitol; photograph taken in April 1865, at the end of the American Civil War

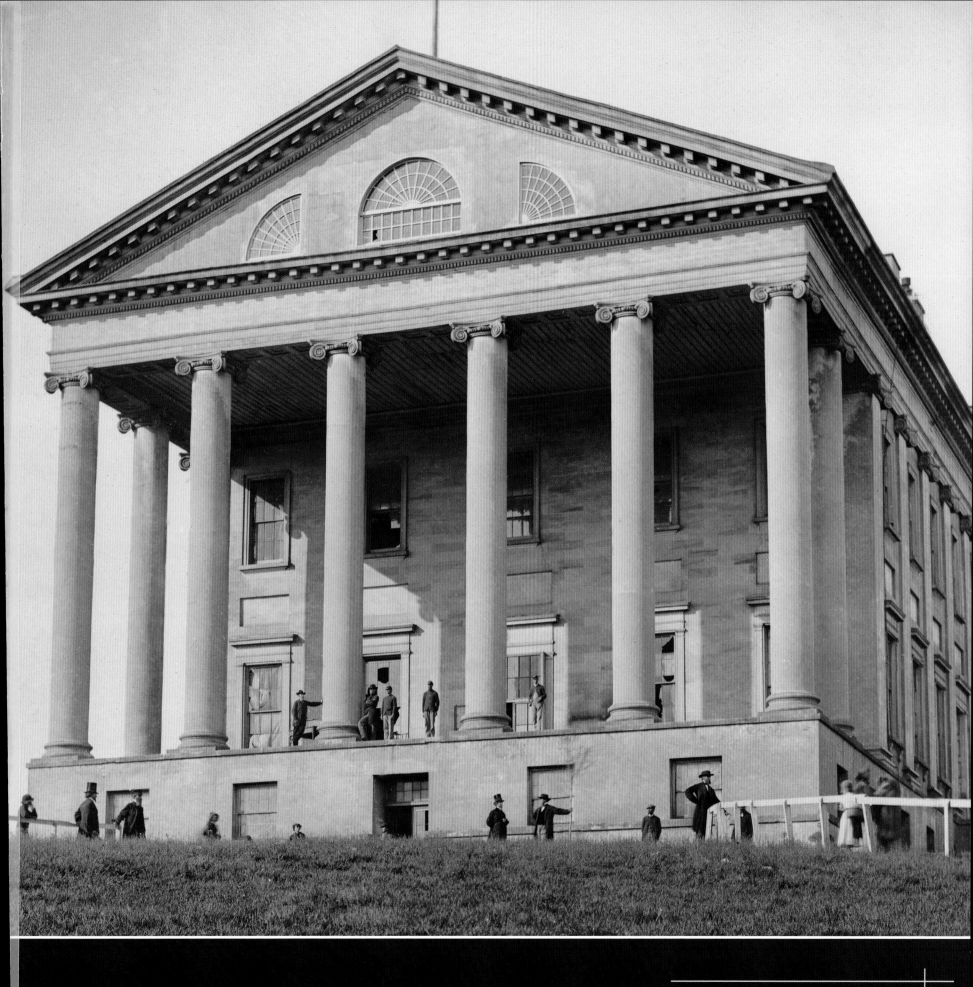

Jefferson later described the Capitol's design:

The capitol is of brick, one hundred and thirty-four feet long, seventy feet wide, and forty-five feet high, exclusive of the basement. Twenty-eight feet of its length is occupied by a portico of the whole breadth of the house, showing its six columns in front, and two intercolumniations in flank. It is of a single order, which is Ionic; its columns four feet two inches in diameter, and their entablature [engraved decoration] running around the whole building. The portico is crowded by a pediment, the height of which is [two-ninths] of its span.

Jefferson knew that time was of the essence in getting the Capitol built. Early in the design process, he was appalled to learn that ground for the building had already been broken—without his plans in place (the legislators were, again, tired of meeting in that old tobacco barn). And Jefferson—3,000 or so miles away from Richmond—also worried about how those plans would be implemented. This was an era before blueprints, and Jefferson knew from his experience in building Monticello that American builders needed a detailed, literal model from which to work.

So Jefferson and Clérisseau commissioned a detailed model of their design from Jean-Pierre Fouquet (1752–1829), who was widely considered one of the greatest architectural-model makers of the era. The model added significantly to the design cost (Jefferson didn't have a big budget to begin with), but as he wrote, it was "absolutely necessary for the guide of workmen not very expert in their art."

Above: The plaster model of the Maison Carrée Jefferson sent to guide work on the Virginia Capitol

Built of plaster of Paris reinforced with iron rods, Fouquet's 1:60-scale model (one inch to every five feet) is an architectural masterpiece in miniature. It was also a kind of marketing tool, serving the additional purpose of impressing the impatient politicians in Richmond that their proposed capitol would be a masterpiece. It also proved to be an invaluable guide for the various renovations the Capitol underwent during the nineteenth and twentieth centuries (Clérisseau's original plans, sent to Richmond in January 1786, went missing in the 1790s).

The actual building of the Capitol took about twelve years—from 1786 to 1798. For much of that time, Jefferson was in Paris or serving as secretary of state and vice president. As a result, he couldn't keep tabs on the construction, and so—Monsieur Fouquet's magnificent model notwithstanding—the original design was somewhat altered. The biggest changes were the addition of a basement for government offices (Jefferson intended these to be housed in an upper story) and the omission of the stairs leading to the portico (the stairs wouldn't be added until a much later renovation).

Still, despite the compromises, Jefferson and Clérisseau achieved their goal of creating a Capitol that translated the grace and balance of an "antient" structure into the soil of the New World. It also established Thomas Jefferson as a public, rather than a purely vernacular, architect. As a visiting French nobleman, the Duc de la Rochefoucault-Liancourt, wrote in 1796, the Capitol—even in its unfinished

The Mysterious "Mr. A. Z."

In an intriguing footnote to architectural history, Jefferson may have submitted his own design for the Presidential Mansion—what would become known as the White House—under an assumed name. In 1792, President George Washington asked for designs for a residence for the Chief Executive, to be built in the planned national capital in the newly established District of Columbia. One of the submissions came from a "Mr. A. Z." Historians speculate that Mr. A. Z. was none other than Washington's own secretary of state—Thomas Jefferson—based on the fact that the plan's drawing style seems similar to Jefferson's, and that the design has a distinctly Palladian look. Jefferson's authorship of the plan has never been fully established, however. Irish-born architect James Hoban ultimately won the competition.

state—was "beyond comparison, the first, the most noble, and the greatest [building] in all America." And it would influence the architecture of the new national capital city rising along the Potomac River—Washington, D.C.

THE CAPITOL AFTER JEFFERSON

Jefferson lived long enough to sense that the unity of the country he had done so much to bring into being was under threat from the issue of slavery. Like many Americans of the Revolutionary era, he hoped that, somehow, slavery would eventually die out in the South. The growing importance of slave-cultivated cotton to the nation's economy, however, dampened that hope.

In 1819, the Missouri Territory, part of the vast stretch of western territory that Jefferson had acquired for the United States in the Louisiana Purchase, applied for statehood—as a state where slavery would be legal. If Missouri was admitted to the Union, the political balance between free and slave states in Congress would be upset and slavery would spread into the West. In an 1820 letter, Jefferson wrote, "[T]his momentous question, like a fire bell in the night, awakened and filled me with terror. I considered it at once as the knell of the Union."

The so-called Compromise of 1820, which admitted Maine as a free state to balance Missouri's admission, and which outlawed slavery below latitude 36° 30′ in the West, solved the "momentous question"—for the moment at least. The Union managed to endure for another four decades until the fire of civil war finally flamed up. After Virginia seceded from the Union in April 1861, Richmond became the capital of the Confederate States of America, and during the Civil War, Jefferson's Capitol served as home to both the Virginia General Assembly and the Confederate Congress. Four years later, much of Richmond was destroyed when Union troops stormed the city, but the Capitol survived intact.

Although intact, even before the Civil War, the Capitol was badly in need of renovation and repair: the Assembly never seemed to find the money for proper upkeep. In 1858, the Assembly commissioned the German-born architect Albert Lybrock (1827–1886) to submit designs for the enlargement and modernization of the building. The plans he offered included finally constructing the front steps that Jefferson and Clérisseau had originally specified, but the war broke out before work could begin and Lybrock's plans were put aside indefinitely.

After the war had ended, the sorry state of the building was demonstrated in dramatic fashion in what would become known as the "Capitol Disaster." On April 27, 1870, spectators crammed into the flimsy second-floor gallery to watch as the

Above: Harper's Weekly's depiction of the 1870 "Capitol Disaster"

Virginia Court of Appeals rendered its decision in a disputed mayoral election. Shortly after 11:00 a.m., the gallery collapsed. *Harper's Weekly* described the event:

> The floor was crushed through as if it had been glass, and, with its mass of human beings, fell into the Hall of Delegates, a cloud of dust rising like smoke from the ruin. The scene was terrible. Through the cloud of dust and plaster that obscured the atmosphere, the horror-stricken survivors could discern nothing but a confused mass of dead and wounded flung together on the floor, while cries and groans arose that none who heard will ever forget.

The disaster killed sixty-two people, and in its aftermath there were calls for the building to be demolished and replaced with a more modern structure. Instead, the Capitol was simply repaired in a slapdash fashion. By the turn of the twentieth century, the Capitol's dilapidated condition was something of a scandal, "a reproach to the State," as Governor Andrew Jackson Montague put it in 1902.

STEPPING SLOWLY

The original Jefferson-Clérisseau plans for the Capitol specified an imposing set of steps leading to the portico, in keeping with Jefferson's vision of the structure as "the Temple on the Hill." However, the contractor hired by Virginia's government, Samuel Dobie, decided to build two relatively small, winding staircases on either side of the portico instead. The modification had a practical purpose (it permitted windows

Left: A Union soldier after the occupation and destruction of Richmond, Virginia, with the Capitol building in the distance, 1865 *Above:* Entrance Hall on the first floor of the Virginia Capitol, 1988

for the building's basement offices), but this change and others made by Dobie aggravated Jefferson, who was trying to manage the project from 3,000 miles away in Paris, at a time when a letter could take weeks, if not months, to cross the Atlantic. The steps that Jefferson had designed were finally incorporated during the Capitol's 1904–1906 reconstruction.

The Assembly finally voted for funding a major renovation, which was carried out from 1904 to 1906 under the direction of architect John Kevan Peebles. The building was totally modernized, including the installation of steel structural reinforcement, an elevator, and telephone wiring. In the course of the renovation, however, the Capitol's original interior was essentially gutted and a number of changes were made to the exterior, including repaving the portico in marble and modifying the columns. Most significantly, Peebles added two entirely new

buildings as chambers for the two branches of the General Assembly, the House of Delegates and the Senate. Peebles came in for some criticism from those who felt that the additions violated the original Jefferson-Clérisseau design; he responded by noting that the wings did not "disturb [any] lines of the present structure" and that given their Classical Revival style, "Mr. Jefferson himself, if he were present, would approve it."

The Capitol underwent another major revamp from 1962 to 1964, during which the hyphens (connecting structures) that linked Peebles's wings to the original structure were enlarged, and again during 2004–2007. The most recent renovation, which cost more than $100 million, was completed just in time for Queen Elizabeth II's state visit to Virginia to commemorate the four-hundredth anniversary of the founding of Jamestown.

Above: Aerial view of the Virginia Capitol and surrounding Richmond, 2004 *Opposite:* Second floor of the Virginia Capitol, c. 1991

CHAPTER 4

JEFFERSON'S RETREAT
POPLAR FOREST
1806–1816

> *"I . . . just returned from Poplar Forest, which I have visited four times this year. I have an excellent house there, inferior only to Monticello, and am comfortably fixed and attended there, and pass my time there in a tranquility and retirement much adapted to my age and indolence."*
>
> —THOMAS JEFFERSON, 1821

Located in Bedford County, Virginia, about ninety miles from Monticello, close to present-day Lynchburg, Poplar Forest was Jefferson's country retreat. This begs the question: Why did Jefferson need another country retreat when he had Monticello?

The answer lies in the changing circumstances of Jefferson's life. He built Monticello I to serve as a family home (although, sadly, it would only fulfill that role for about a decade) at a time when, despite his prominence in Virginia, he was still essentially a private citizen. By the time Monticello II neared completion in the first decade of the nineteenth century, he was in his second term as president and famous throughout America and Europe as a statesman and "polymath." This resulted in a constant stream of visitors showing up at the door clutching "letters of introduction"—or just showing up, period. Monticello II, in fact, functioned kind of as a modern presidential library/museum . . . with the former president in more or less permanent residence.

Left: View of the house at Poplar Forest from southwest *Left, inset:* Jefferson portrait, 1805

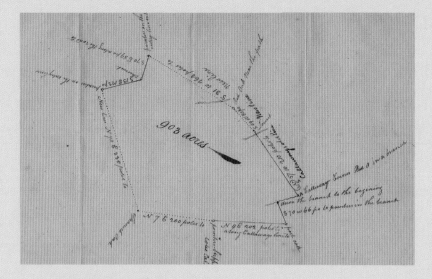

Furthermore, Monticello II—as the centerpiece of a community the size of a small town—was a busy and bustling place, full of the sound of blacksmiths hammering nails, the smells of cooking wafting up from the "dependencies," and so on, all of which served to distract Jefferson from his beloved books, his correspondence, and his experiments. Like Monticello, Poplar Forest was a working plantation as well as a residence, but it offered the former president considerably more peace and quiet than he could get at his primary home. As his granddaughter Ellen Randolph Coolidge put it in a letter written in the 1850s, "At Poplar Forest [Jefferson] found a pleasant home, rest, and leisure [and] power to carry on his favorite pursuits—to think, to study, to read."

From about 1806 until the early 1820s—when he became too aged and frail to make the two-and-a-half day-carriage ride from Monticello to Poplar Forest—Jefferson would slip away to the latter several times a year to refresh his mind, body, and spirit in a house whose grounds were shaded by those eponymous tulip poplar trees. His stays there ranged from a couple of weeks to a couple of months in length.

The house at Poplar Forest was the product of a mature, considered mind; Jefferson was already in his sixties by the time he began it. By then he'd absorbed a variety of influences and filtered them through the lens of his own architectural vision. So Poplar Forest is, perhaps, the most wholly individualistic of all Jefferson's designs.

The Capitol at Richmond and the Academical Village at the University of Virginia were public buildings, and Monticello II was intended, at least partly, as a kind of "statement." But Jefferson renovated a new house at Poplar Forest with little

but his own enjoyment in mind. He underscored its private nature in an 1812 letter: "When finished, [Poplar Forest] will be the best dwelling house in the state, except that of Monticello; perhaps preferable to that, as more proportioned to the faculties of a private citizen."

Jefferson acquired the roughly 5,000-acre Poplar Forest in 1773 as an inheritance upon the death of his father-in-law. For the next three decades Jefferson was mostly an absentee landlord, relying on the property's wheat and tobacco fields for income.

In 1781, Poplar Forest became a literal retreat for Jefferson when he and his family fled Monticello a few steps ahead of the British. They stayed there for a couple of months, living in the overseer's house. For much of this time he was laid up by injuries he received when his horse threw him. (In a fitting twist, the horse's name was Caractacus—after the first-century-CE Briton who rallied his countrymen to oppose Roman occupation.) Jefferson used this involuntary downtime to write *Notes on the State of Virginia*, which would be published in Paris five years later. (Contrary to the self-effacing statement in the quote that prefaces this chapter, Jefferson was never indolent.) Jefferson's brief exile at Poplar Forest, however, may have led him to consider the plantation as a potential site for a future home. According to Jefferson's *Garden Books*, he arranged for various species of fruit trees and flowers to be planted on the property around this time.

In any event, actual construction didn't begin until 1806. Jefferson relied on many of the same artisans—slave and free—who'd built Monticello II. John Hemings, assisted by two of Sally Hemings's sons, was chiefly responsible for the carpentry, both on the exterior and interior. Hugh Chisholm oversaw the brickwork—which Jefferson wasn't entirely happy with at first, as he made clear in an 1807 letter to the craftsman. Richard Barry, the painter, and John and Reuben Perry, the carpenters, also contributed. Because work on Monticello II was simultaneous with the construction of Poplar Forest, many elements of the latter—such as windows and doors—came out of the former's workshops.

Preoccupied with the presidency, Jefferson only managed to visit the Poplar Forest building site a handful of times; but as with Monticello II, he kept tabs on things by letter. The house was ready for occupancy by the time Jefferson left Washington, D.C., but as with both Monticellos, it was never really finished. Work on the interior continued for several more years: a one-hundred-foot-long service wing comparable to one of the "dependencies" at Monticello II wasn't done until 1814, and Jefferson was ordering additional exterior decoration as late as the 1820s.

Above: Survey of 903-acre plat of part of Poplar Forest detailing coordinates

The house that Jefferson first slept in in 1809 was, like Monticello, of brick construction with wood trim. Instead of the terrace-topped "dependencies" at Monticello II, Jefferson achieved symmetry by placing two conical earthen mounds—by-products of the excavation required for the lower floor—on either side of the main structure. These mounds were planted with trees and bushes. Later, a service wing was added to the east side of the house, giving the whole an L shape—Hugh Howard describes the wing's aesthetic effect as being like "the outrigger on a canoe"—while a double row of mulberry trees added balance on the west side.

A circular carriageway enclosed the house and provided the approach to its formal entrance, the North Portico. In typical Jeffersonian style, the portico was pedimented with a lunette window, and graced by four columns of the Tuscan order, topped by a "Chinese railing" similar to the ones found atop the flanking pavilions at Monticello II. Interestingly, the North and South porticoes (Ellen Randolph Coolidge described the latter as a "verhandah") appear to be something of an afterthought. Jefferson only specified them in the same September 1806 letter in which he ordered Hugh Chisholm to construct the stairways.

THE INTERIOR

Much of what we know of Poplar Forest in Jefferson's time comes from the reminiscences of one of his granddaughters, Ellen Randolph Coolidge. In 1856, she described the house's layout:

> [The house] was of brick, one storey in front, and, owing to the falling of the ground, two in the rear. It was an . . . octagon, with a centre-hall twenty feet square, lighted from above. This was a beautiful room, and served as a dining-room. Round it were grouped a bright drawing-room [the Parlor] looking south, my grandfather's own chamber, three other bedrooms, and a pantry. A terrace extended from one side of the house; there was a portico in front connected by a vestibule to the central room,; [*sic*] and in the rear a verhandah [*sic*], on which the drawing room opened, with its windows to the floor.

The plan of the main floor contrasts in many ways with that of Monticello II and reflects Poplar Forest's more intimate nature. For one thing, there was no "filtering

Left, top: Brickwork on the South Portico, 1986 *Left, bottom:* The Parlor at Poplar Forest, 1940 *Enclosures:* Jefferson's plans and description of Poplar Forest: sketch of the service quarters, c. 1805; letter from Jefferson to Benjamin Rush describing daily activities at Poplar Forest, August 17, 1811; plans for the kitchens and service quarters with notes on the measurements, 1805

space" like the Indian Hall at Monticello II, just a narrow hallway, flanked by two Bedchambers, that led from the North Portico to the Dining Room. In this, Jefferson anticipated Frank Lloyd Wright, whose designs often featured low passageways opening up into high-ceilinged spaces.

The Dining Room was at the center of the house. Its dimensions formed a perfect cube—twenty feet in width, height, and depth. Because there were no windows, light came from a skylight—not quite a rotunda, but close. (The skylight—probably the largest in America at the time—was shattered by a hailstorm in 1819 but later rebuilt.) As befitting the most formal room in an informal house, Jefferson specified the Doric order for the room's decoration, with a frieze based on the Roman Baths of Diocletian. Characteristically, though, Jefferson modified the classical order, adding ox skulls to the decorative scheme: "I can indulge in my own case, although in a public work I feel bound to follow authority strictly," he wrote. When the sculptor he hired protested at this violation of the purity of the order, Jefferson told him, "You are right . . . those of the Baths of Diocletian are all human faces. . . . But in my middle room at Poplar Forest I mean to mix the faces and ox-skulls."

Beyond the Dining Room was the Parlor, where the decoration was in the Ionic order. It also had an "antient" model—the Roman temple of Fortuna Virilis—although, just as he modified the frieze in the Dining Room, Jefferson added more ox skulls and *putti* (cherubs) here.

The Parlor led to the South Portico, which was accessed via both a double door and four triple-hung sash windows—the latter yet another typical Jefferson touch. The lower two sashes could be raised to form additional doorways to the Portico, allowing more light and air. The South Portico overlooked a *parterre*, or sunken garden, and an expansive lawn.

Connecting doors on either side of the Dining Room led to a Pantry and a Bedchamber on one side and two additional Bedchambers on the other. That was

Above: Poplar Forest's North Portico, 1986

drawn by C.J.R.
"Poplar Forest"

drawn by C. J. Randolph
"Poplar Forest"

it for the main floor; Poplar Forest had a mere eight main rooms, in contrast to the thirty-plus rooms that comprised Monticello II. And there was no sequestered private space comparable to Jefferson's personal quarters at his primary residence. (Jefferson did have an "air-closet"—indoor toilet—installed adjacent to his Bedchamber; it was the only such facility in the Poplar Forest house.)

So, in Poplar Forest's design, Jefferson largely did away with the distinction between personal and private, formal and informal spaces that characterized the floor plan of Monticello II. But he did make use of some of the innovations found at Monticello II—including alcove beds, which Jefferson prized for their space-saving quality. He also installed another polygraph in the Parlor at Poplar Forest. Jefferson did a lot of his reading and writing in that room, taking advantage of its glorious southern light.

Not much is known about Poplar Forest's furnishings—at least in comparison to what is known about those of Monticello. In Ellen Randolph Coolidge's words, "It was furnished in the simplest manner, but had a very tasty air, [and] there was nothing common or second-rate about any part of the establishment, though there was no appearance of expense." We know that for seating, the rooms contained some of the famous Windsor chairs produced in England, as well as items Jefferson brought back from France in 1789. Modern archaeological research on the site has turned up fragments of fine porcelain and china—evidence of the owner's refined tastes.

Refined tastes notwithstanding, Poplar Forest fulfilled its owner's craving for the simple life (as he conceived it) and a place to bask in the company of his family—especially his granddaughters Ellen and Cornelia Randolph. Jefferson doted on them and on his great-grandchildren (the first of whom arrived in 1810) as well. "It is only with them," he once said of the young folks to a visitor, "that a grave man can play the fool."

Ellen first visited the house with her sister Cornelia in 1816. They arrived in Jefferson's landau-style carriage, which was equipped with one of his beloved gadgets—an odometer that rang a bell every mile.

Decades later, Ellen wrote that she and her sister would "[Make Jefferson's] tea, preside over his dinner table, accompany him in his walks, in his occasional drives, and be with him at the time he most enjoyed society, from tea time till bed time."

Opposite, top and bottom: Ink and wash drawings created by Jefferson's granddaughter Cornelia Randolph while visiting Poplar Forest *Right:* The Parlor at Poplar Forest with triple-sash windows and the interior glass doors

Jefferson and the Sash Window

Jefferson didn't invent the sash window—the English scientist Robert Hooke (1635–1703) is generally credited with that—but he pioneered its use in American homes at Monticello and Poplar Forest. Previously, windows in European and American buildings were generally fixed in place, but sash windows could be raised and lowered vertically to improve ventilation and increase the amount of natural light reaching the interior. Jefferson designed louvered blinds to go with Monticello's sash windows, writing that "T[he blinds] open back on hinges as in the winter we want both the light and warmth of the sun."

POPLAR FOREST AFTER JEFFERSON

Of all Jefferson's major designs, Poplar Forest remained the most obscure until recently. Just a few decades ago, some Jeffersonian scholars believed that the house was "no longer in existence." But it did still exist—if barely. About the time Jefferson turned eighty and decided he was too frail to make the journey from Monticello, he turned Poplar Forest over to his grandson, Francis Eppes. Two years after Jefferson died in 1826, Eppes sold the property. In 1845, a fire left Poplar Forest a gutted shell. (The fire may have been facilitated by flaws in Jefferson's design—the house had fifteen fireplaces but only four chimneys.) The house was rebuilt by its then-owner, Edward Hutter, but in the Greek Revival style popular at the time. Inside and out, the Hutter version bore little resemblance to Jefferson's country retreat.

Poplar Forest changed hands several more times (and went through a mid-twentieth-century renovation, including the installation of electrical wiring and indoor plumbing) before the nonprofit Corporation for Poplar Forest bought it in 1984. The Corporation was a genuine grass-roots effort that began with a small group of local residents; elementary students raised the money, which provided funds for the labor that allowed Poplar Forest to be opened to the public, for the first time, in 1986.

Since 1993, a carefully researched (and still ongoing) restoration has been underway, accompanied by extensive archaeological investigations of the house and grounds. In 1998, the project won the prestigious Honor Award from the National Trust for Historic Preservation. The restoration is challenging because so few plans and views of the original structure survive, so Jefferson's many letters to his builders and artisans have proved invaluable in recreating the country dwelling.

The home that was once thought to have faded into the Virginia landscape is proving, in the twenty-first century, to be a great resource in establishing Thomas Jefferson's architectural legacy. In historian David McCullough's words:

> It is becoming clear how very important Poplar Forest is to our enlarged understanding of Thomas Jefferson and the reach of his imagination. That Jefferson was, along with so many other things, one of the premier American architects, has been long appreciated, but the originality and ingenuity of Poplar Forest—especially now that it is being so superbly restored—raise his standing still higher. This is an American masterpiece by a great American artist who also happened to be President of the United States.

Left: View of Poplar Forest from the southeast showing a service wing, 1986

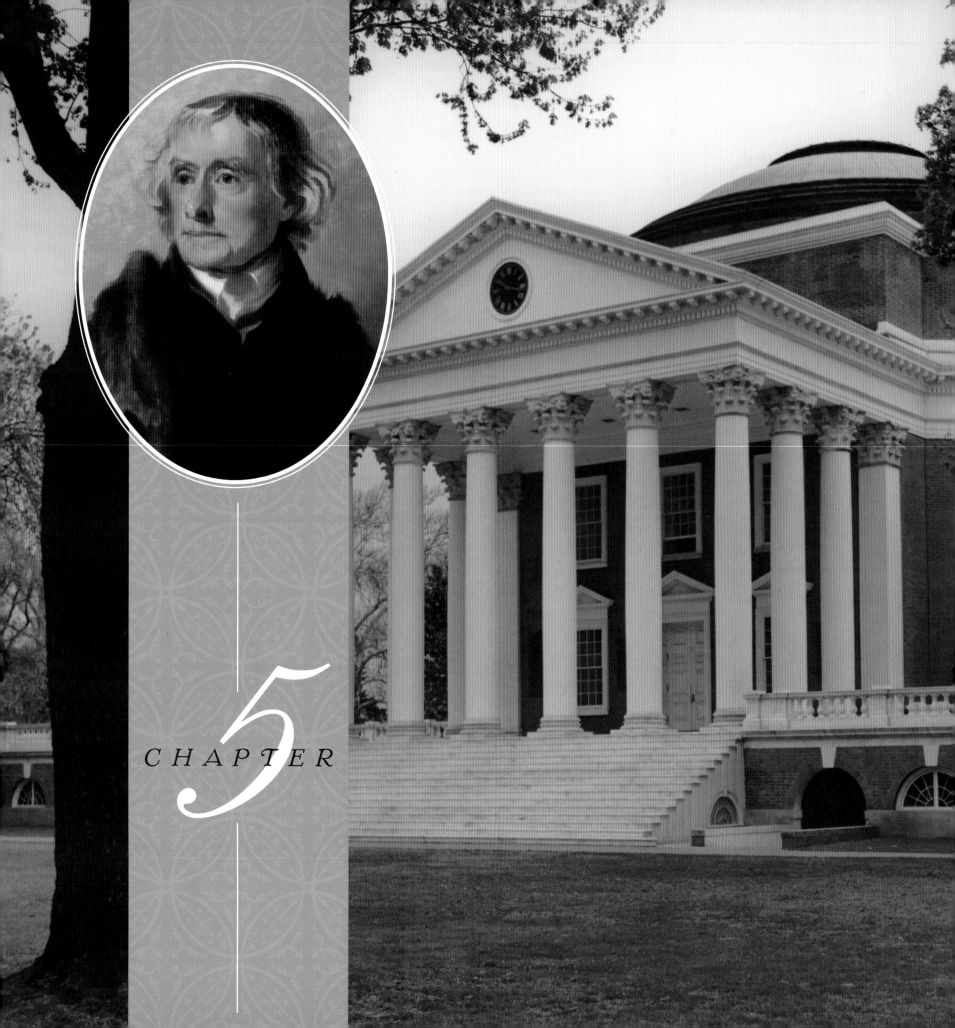

CHAPTER

5

THE UNIVERSITY OF VIRGINIA

1817-1826

> "*We wish to establish in the upper country of Virginia, and more centrally for the State, a University on a plan so broad and liberal and modern, as to be worth patronizing with the public support, and be a temptation to the youth of other States to come and drink of the cup of knowledge and fraternize with us.*"
>
> —THOMAS JEFFERSON, 1800

On the afternoon of November 4, 1824, a carriage bearing a very distinguished—and most welcome—visitor came up the drive at Monticello to visit Thomas Jefferson. It was the Marquis de Lafayette. Nearly fifty years before, the nobleman—then a teenaged French army officer on fire with the ideals of liberty—had come to America to help in its fight for independence. Now a sixty-seven-year-old hero of both the American and French

Left: The Rotunda at the University of Virginia, c. 1950s *Left, inset:* Portrait of Jefferson at age seventy-eight, 1821

Revolutions, he'd returned to America for a final visit. The two old comrades had a lot to talk about, obviously. But the eighty-one-year-old Jefferson was no doubt especially brimming with pride at what would take place the next day.

On November 5, the two old revolutionaries traveled a few miles to a twenty-eight-acre tract of rolling land just outside the small town of Charlottesville. The occasion was the inaugural ceremony of the University of Virginia. Four hundred guests gathered for a banquet in the Rotunda, the (still unfinished) building that would serve as the library and architectural centerpiece of the campus. At the conclusion of the banquet, Lafayette rose and offered a toast to Jefferson as "the founder of the University of Virginia." Jefferson wept.

The first students—just forty or so of them—wouldn't arrive to start classes for another five months, but the banquet was an exquisite moment of validation for Jefferson. For decades he had planned a public university for his beloved Virginia. Now in his old age he'd see his longtime dream become a reality.

"The hobby of my old age," as Jefferson called the university, also represented the culmination of Jefferson's career as an architect. In the opinion of some architectural historians, it's his finest and most enduring design.

Like all of his great designs, it reflected the man and his philosophy. Monticello was Jefferson's ideal of a private residence; the Capitol at Richmond was his ideal for a "seat of government"; and the campus of the University of Virginia was a physical embodiment of his ideas about education and the transforming role he wanted it to play for both his native state and for the new nation: "I hope [the University of Virginia] will prove a blessing to my own state, and not unuseful perhaps to some others," he wrote in an 1820 letter.

The design for the university also drew together the two great strands of Jefferson's architectural thinking, which had been percolating in his mind since he produced his first drawings for Monticello I as a young man: a due respect for the classical past, suitably adapted to the American landscape, combined with a completely original vision in keeping with a young country that had thrown off Old World traditions and customs. The University of Virginia would be an institution, in his words, free of "the restraint imposed in other seminaries by the shackles of a domineering hierarchy and a bigoted adhesion to ancient habits."

The beautiful set of buildings that would arise near Charlottesville wasn't exclusively Jefferson's creation. Jefferson turned for help to the English-born architect Benjamin Latrobe (1764–1820), whom he had appointed "Surveyor of Public

Left: Wood engraving of Marquis de Lafayette, c. 1778-1880

Buildings" during his presidential administration, and, to a lesser extent, to William Thornton (1759–1828), designer of the U.S. Capitol in Washington, D.C. In addition, several of Jefferson's gang of trusted and talented craftsmen from Monticello and Poplar Forest—James Dinsmore, John Neilson, and John Perry—contributed not only to the construction but also to the design. Just who was responsible for what is hard to determine because many of the original plans have vanished. Architectural historians have credited the design of some of the structures to these individuals; others are considered composites or collaborations.

But, as with all of his great projects, the overall vision was pure Jefferson.

TOWARD THE ACADEMICAL VILLAGE

Jefferson was passionate on the subject of education. He was one of history's great autodidacts, mastering language after language and subject after subject—from locksmithing to astronomy—through endless and energetic reading and doing. He'd had the benefit of formal higher education, too, at the College of William and Mary, at a time when such an education was open to only a tiny percentage of Americans—almost all of them, like Jefferson, upper-class white males.

When the United States came into being, the idea of free, compulsory, public education was still decades in the future, but Jefferson was an early advocate. As he wrote to his mentor George Wythe in 1786, "No other sure foundation can be devised for the preservation of freedom." As governor of Virginia in the late 1770s, Jefferson tried to enact an ambitious statewide educational program, which would guarantee instruction in the basics to "all free children, male and female," and a system of higher education "without regard to wealth, birth, or accidental condition or circumstance." (The significance of the word "free" here is obvious, and as far as higher education went, Jefferson, like most men of his time, didn't think women needed any education beyond the basics.) Jefferson's zeal for educational reform was probably augmented by the fact that literacy rates in Virginia and the rest of the South seriously lagged behind those of New England and the middle states.

Political opposition and lack of funding meant that Jefferson's visionary plans were only adopted in a lackluster fashion. He kept trying—especially for the establishment of a state university for Virginia. By early 1800, when he was vice president, Jefferson was working out the details. His determination to build what he called "the great state university" intensified during his presidency when he failed in his efforts to create a national university.

Above: Painting of Benjamin H. Latrobe, c. 1804

But it wasn't until his retirement from government that he could finally get on with his self-described "hobby." In 1816, the Virginia General Assembly finally passed a bill authorizing the creation of a university—originally called the Central College—and appropriating funds to buy a parcel of land at Monroe Hill, so named because it had once been owned by another prominent Virginian, James Monroe, who would be in the White House when the first students finally arrived.

Jefferson introduced a number of then-radical concepts for the planned university. Its curriculum wouldn't be limited to the traditional trilogy of Law, Medicine, and Religion, but would also include Astronomy, Architecture, Botany, Philosophy, and Political Science. Students wouldn't be required to follow a set course of classes; instead, each student would be free "to attend the schools of his choice and no other than he chooses." This was the birth of the "elective system" in American higher education. And Jefferson didn't want the faculty to be remote figures, aloof from the day-to-day life of the student body—students and faculty would share the same living spaces.

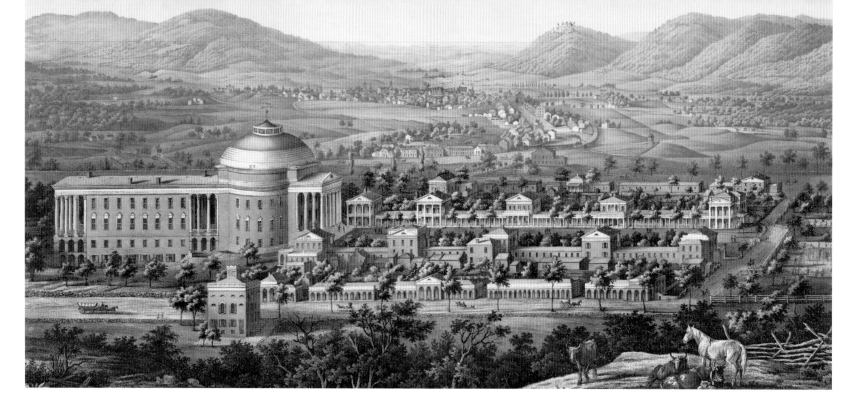

The design of the campus reflected these innovations. Jefferson drew up a basic plan for the university in 1814. It would create what he termed an "Academical Village." It was a departure from traditional university layouts. The universities that had emerged in medieval Europe—Padua and Bologna in Italy, Oxford in England, and so forth—were originally intended to educate young men for a lifetime in the clergy. For this reason they tended to be inward-facing, with college buildings fully enclosing a quadrangle—similar to the cloisters in which monks lived, worked, and prayed.

For his New World university, Jefferson instead planned a U shape, with ten Pavilions—five on each side—anchored by "some central building," with the whole enclosing a green space on three sides. (In its final form, this 200-foot-wide expanse would be known as "the Lawn.") But the south end of the Lawn was left open, to take in views of the surrounding hills. As with his hilltop homes at Monticello and Poplar Forest, and the Virginia Capitol on Shockhoe Hill overlooking the James River, Jefferson wanted the eyes to be opened to the expansive American landscape and the mind to be opened to the limitless possibilities it offered.

As always, Jefferson mixed the practical with the philosophical. As early as 1804, he'd written, "In fact an [sic] University should not be an [sic] house but a village." He was thinking about his own alma mater, William and Mary. There, the living and teaching spaces were crammed into a single building. This made the college vulnerable to two of the great scourges of the time—fire and communicable diseases. Spreading things out would reduce these risks. Again, Jefferson wanted it "light and airy."

Work on the Academical Village began in the summer of 1817; Jefferson himself placed the surveyor's stakes. As he did, perhaps he thought of his father, mapping the Virginia wilderness. Now Jefferson was laying out not only a physical space, but also a new frontier for the American mind.

Above: Printing of the University of Virginia and surrounding area, including Charlottesville and Monticello, 1856 *Background:* Plan for a "Hotel" at the university *Flap:* Page from Jefferson's 1783 *Catalog of Books* outlining the "faculties of the mind" *Opposite:* Engraving of Jefferson's Academical Village, 1826

The Rotunda

Soon there were a couple hundred workmen swarming around the site—some brought in from Monticello, others hired from as far away as Philadelphia. But as work on the Academical Village progressed, a question remained—what would the "central building" be?

It would most definitely not be a chapel—a structure that was often the most prominent building in the colleges of European universities and their colonial American counterparts. Every other American college founded up to this time had some religious affiliation; the first (Harvard, founded in 1636) was originally intended to educate Puritan divines, and William and Mary produced ministers for the Anglican Church—a denomination that was "established" in colonial Virginia, in the sense that it was being supported by public funds.

Jefferson was adamant that the public university be firmly secular in character. This was in keeping with his lifelong attitude toward religion. Like many men of the Enlightenment, Jefferson was a Deist—someone who, while perhaps acknowledging the existence of some kind of Supreme Being, rejected the "superstitions" and formal practices of organized religion. And on a political level, he believed deeply in the separation of church and state.

In 1786, while in Europe, Jefferson had orchestrated the adoption of the Virginia Statute for Religious Freedom, which removed taxpayer support for the Anglican Church and declared "That no man shall be compelled to frequent or support any religious worship, place, or ministry whatsoever . . . but that all men shall be free to profess, and by argument to maintain, their opinion in matters of religion, and that the same shall in no wise [sic] diminish, enlarge, or affect their civil capacities." The statute had a direct influence on the First Amendment of the Constitution's Bill of Rights.

Jefferson wasn't entirely hostile to religion. He showed an interest in Unitarianism—which rejected the traditional Christian doctrine of the Trinity—a movement founded by his friend, the great English scientist Joseph Priestley, who'd fled to America in 1794 following persecution for his radical political and religious beliefs. In 1820, Jefferson published a cut-and-paste version of the New Testament—it kept Jesus's moral teachings, but omitted references to phenomena like miracles, virgin birth, and the resurrection.

So there would be no chapel in Jefferson's original version of the university, let alone any School of Divinity. He put this quite plainly in an 1814 letter: "a professorship of theology should have no place in our institution." In the curriculum, religion

Above: The Rotunda at the UVA, 1890 *Flap, front:* Panoramic view of the University, 1898 *Flap, back:* The Lawn at the UVA, c. 2007 *Opposite:* Stairs leading up to the Rotunda, c. 1990

74   THOMAS JEFFERSON: ARCHITECT

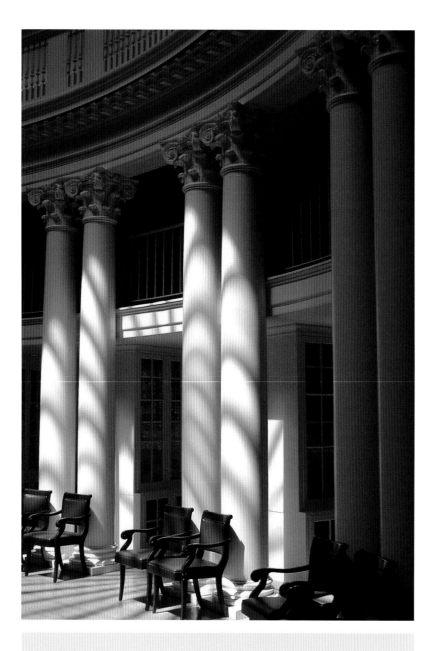

The Planetarium That Wasn't

Jefferson originally wanted the upper space of the Rotunda, beneath the dome, to serve as a space for the study of astronomy—it was to "be painted sky blue and spangled with . . . gilt stars in their position and magnitude copied exactly from any selected hemisphere of our latitude." A professor would sit in a movable seat—operated by pulleys—to point out different celestial bodies to students. For reasons unknown, Jefferson's plan was never implemented; if it had been, the space would have been the first planetarium in the United States.

would be taught in the context of ethics and philosophy. He retained the suspicion that organized religion was unalterably opposed to the kind of free inquiry he wanted to flourish at Charlottesville. As he wrote to another good friend and frequent guest at Monticello, the Portuguese diplomat José Correa de Serra, in 1820: "The priests of the different religious sects . . . dread the advance of science as witches do the approach of daylight."

Ultimately, the focal point of the Academical Village would be a library—a temple not to religion but, in Jefferson's words, to "the authority of nature and power of reason." And once again Palladio's influence surfaces. Though Jefferson never made it to Rome during his time in Europe, he was familiar with the ancient Pantheon (the "temple of all the gods") from the drawings in Palladio's *The Four Books of Architecture*. The original Pantheon structure was built around 30 BCE by Marcus Vipsanius Agrippa, the same soldier/statesman responsible for the Maison Carrée, the inspiration for the Virginia Capitol in Richmond. It burned down around 80 CE but was later reconstructed down to the last detail during the reign of Emperor Hadrian from 117–138 CE.

Jefferson scaled down the design to fit the site; his plan called for a structure about half the size of the Roman Pantheon. It also appears that the plan for the building was very much a collaboration between Jefferson and Latrobe.

In the library's final form—it wasn't completed until after Jefferson's death—it became known as the Rotunda, from its cylindrical shape and from the oculus that (as at Monticello II) flooded the interior—which originally consisted of three main elliptical rooms—with natural light. It featured the usual Jeffersonian pedimented portico, and a portico with Corinthian columns. And, as at Monticello, Jefferson designed a special Dome Room—in this case, for the study of astronomy. It was supposed to have movable mechanical models of the sun, moon, stars, and planets.

With the Rotunda's interior, Jefferson indulged his passion for saving space. He intended the building to do double duty as a place for meetings and social events, so the library stacks were recessed behind columns. This was the bibliographical equivalent of the alcove beds at Monticello and Poplar Forest. Jefferson's obsessive-compulsive attention to detail was also evident in the design of the Rotunda's interior; for the pine flooring, he specified wood from trees grown at specific latitudes.

Left: Paired columns in the Rotunda with light shining down through the oculus *Enclosures:* Plans for the Rotunda: Southern elevation and lateral section, 1819; first-floor plan, 1823; second-floor plan with notes reducing the dimensions of the Pantheon for the Rotunda, 1823 *Opposite:* Interior of the Rotunda showing the book stacks behind a statue of Thomas Jefferson, c. 1910

Not long after the ground breaking, Jefferson expanded the university plan to include two rows of dining halls—or "hotels," as he called them—behind and in parallel with the Pavilions. The space between the "East Range" and "West Range," as they were designated, allowed Jefferson to indulge in another of his passions—gardening.

Curvy brick walls enclosed six gardens, allowing the cultivation of "pinks and a thousand other flowers, the remaining part[s] planted with beans, peas, cabbage, and many other articles," in the words of one early visitor, plus fruit trees and ornamental shrubs. Besides being pleasing to the eye and providing vegetables for the hotel kitchens, Jefferson believed the gardens would be conducive to the life of the mind—as he put it, "[They] would afford the quiet retirement so friendly to study." The twentieth-century British cultural critic Sir Kenneth Clark noted that the gardens had "something of the quality of a Japanese temple."

Even though architectural historians still debate which individual was responsible for the design of some of the Pavilions, together the Pavilions, the Gardens, the Lawn, and the Rotunda formed a harmonious whole that was immediately acclaimed. George Ticknor of Massachusetts, who visited the Academical Village as it neared completion, declared the university superior to Harvard, writing that its design was "more appropriate to an [sic] university than [any other that] can be found, perhaps, in the world."

Above: A Hotel in the West Range at the University of Virginia

THE UNIVERSITY AFTER JEFFERSON

Virginia's General Assembly formally chartered the university in 1819, and Jefferson hoped that the first students would be admitted the following year. But the inevitable construction delays and financial wrangling with the Assembly delayed the first matriculation until March 1825. Then there was the problem of recruiting faculty. Academics at the established American colleges balked at the prospect of moving to Virginia, so five of the eight original professors were imported from Europe.

Jefferson's involvement with his "hobby" went far beyond overall conception and architectural design. He spent his last years as rector—chief administrator—of the university, and, in Willard Randall's words, in that capacity "he personally drew up class schedules, student rules, and faculty bylaws, and handled a host of other administrative duties, all ratified by a Board of Visitors." (This was the official title of the university's governing body.)

Jefferson didn't provide much of a disciplinary system for the university's student body; he expected that the students, being young gentlemen in an "institution [based] on the illimitable freedom of the human mind," would govern themselves. But . . . college students will be college students. Many members of the university's first class proved more interested in drinking, gambling, and pranking their professors than in debating the finer points of Plato and John Locke.

The students got so out of hand that Jefferson, now a frail eighty-two-year-old, had to visit the campus to restore order. Several students (including one of Jefferson's own nephews) were expelled, others reprimanded, and Jefferson belatedly came up with a student code of conduct. Jefferson was certainly saddened by this turn of events, but he remained completely devoted to the university for the remainder of his life. Every Sunday, for example, he had students come to dinner at Monticello. (Among those who enjoyed the incomparable pleasures of Jefferson's table and conversation was the young Edgar Allan Poe, who spent about a year at the university before dropping out due to money troubles.) And the last building Jefferson ever designed—an Anatomical Theatre for medical studies—was under construction when he died in 1826. A decade later, the university added a School of Engineering and Applied Science—the first such university-affiliated school in the United States. It was a development that, no doubt, would have pleased Jefferson.

Left: The serpentine garden wall at UVA, 1986 *Enclosures:* Plans for the University of Virginia: elevation with three floor plans for Pavilion I with notes on the backside; plans for the Pavilion and Dormitories with a drawing of the U-shape building layout on the backside, 1814 *Opposite:* A statue of Jefferson in the Rotunda, 1989

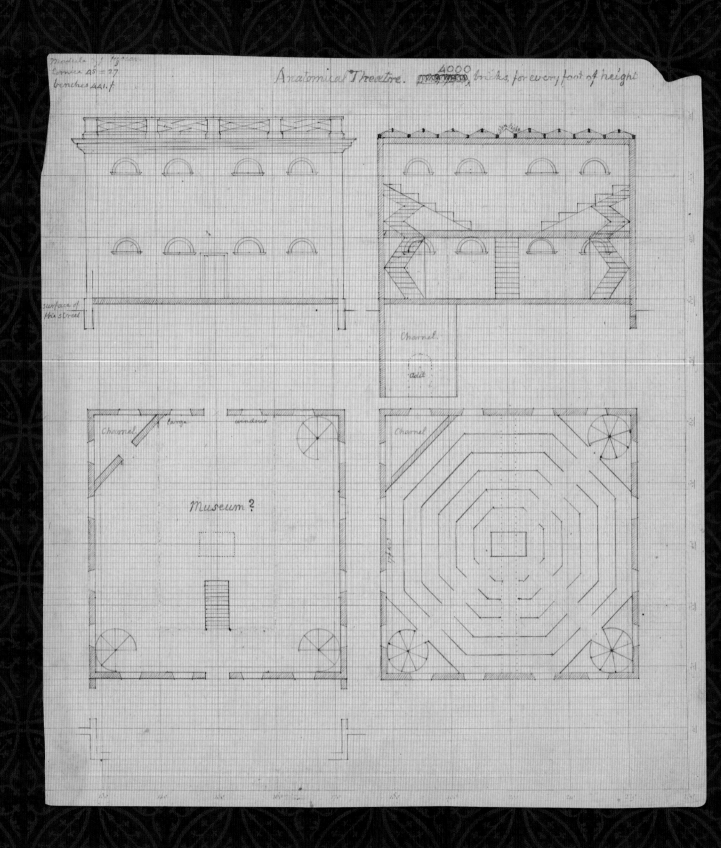

Anatomical Theatre.

Museum?

Charnel.

Charnel.

Charnel.

The university remained open during the Civil War, quite an achievement considering the fighting that raged throughout northern Virginia. In March 1865, with the end of the conflict nearing, Union troops occupied the campus and engaged in some vandalism. But—at the urging of students and faculty—the bluecoats refrained from torching the place.

The Academical Village remained much as Jefferson and his associates had envisioned until October 1895, when fire—that scourge of Jefferson's architectural heritage—consumed the Rotunda and damaged some of the other buildings. Matters weren't helped when, in a failed effort to create a firebreak, the university staff deployed dynamite around the Rotunda. (Students managed to save a full-size statue of Jefferson, which had stood in the Rotunda since 1861, from the flame— it is still there today.)

For the rebuilding of the Rotunda, the university's Board of Visitors commissioned the celebrated New York architectural firm of McKim, Mead, and White. Their version of the Rotunda would deviate considerably from Jefferson's original design; just as John Kevan Peebles defended his twentieth-century changes to the Virginia Capitol as in keeping with Jefferson's vision, Stanford White said that his design was "[one] that Jefferson would unquestionably have adopted . . . could he have directed the restoration"—a statement that Jefferson scholars have criticized. The decade-long restoration also resulted in the construction of three new major buildings for the university. While fine structures in their own right, they were sited at the south end of the Lawn, turning it into an actual quadrangle and eclipsing the view of the surrounding hills that Jefferson had made a part of his original plan.

Left: Study of first- and second-floor plans, east elevation, and section for the last building Jefferson ever designed: The Anatomical Theatre, 1825 *Above:* The UVA's Rotunda and Pavilions at dusk, 1991

In the 1970s, Frederick Doveton Nichols oversaw the restoration of the Rotunda back to its Jeffersonian state—at least as far as it could be determined—and in the 1980s, the university undertook a respectful modernization/restoration of the Pavilions. In 1987, the Academical Village shared with Monticello the great distinction of being named a UNESCO World Heritage Site.

Today, Charlottesville is a city of more than 40,000 people, and the university—with an enrollment of nearly 20,000—sprawls across some 680 acres. But Jefferson's Academical Village remains at its heart. A handful of students—lucky seniors—still live in its Pavilions, although the structures now rarely house faculty and only a couple include classroom space.

The university certainly fulfilled Jefferson's hopes; it is now one of America's finest research universities, and competition for admission is fierce. In a bit of irony that Jefferson might or might not have appreciated, the university also boasts a highly regarded Religious Studies department. It has also had a chapel since 1890—though it is nondenominational.

Jefferson's pride in his Academical Village can be seen in the epitaph he wrote for his own headstone in the graveyard at Monticello. There's no mention of his tenure as first secretary of state, his two-term presidency, or the Louisiana Purchase. Instead, from a lifetime of hyper-achievement, Jefferson singled out just three accomplishments:

HERE WAS BURIED THOMAS JEFFERSON
AUTHOR OF THE DECLARATION OF AMERICAN INDEPENDENCE
OF THE STATUTE OF VIRGINIA FOR RELIGIOUS FREEDOM
AND FATHER OF THE UNIVERSITY OF VIRGINIA

Above: The chapel at the University of Virginia, 2006 *Opposite:* A statue of Thomas Jefferson at the university, 1998

TRANSCRIPTIONS

Page 14
The Four Books on Architecture

(English translation)

Regina Virtvs

The Four Books On Architecture
By Andrea Palladio

In which, after a brief discourse on the five orders and on those rules [avertimento] which are essential to building, private houses, streets, bridges, squares, xysti, and temples are discussed.
Con Privilegi

In Venice, at the printing house of Dominico de' Franceschi. 1570.

Page 18
Garden Books

(page 1, front)
1766. Shadwell.
Mar. 30. Purple hyacinth begins to bloom.
Apr. 6. Narcissus and Puckoon open.
13. Puckoon flowers fallen.
16. A bluish colored, funnel-formed flower in lowgrounds in bloom.
30. Purple flag blooms. Hyacinth & Narcissus gone.
May. 4. Wild honeysuckle in our woods open. —also the Dwarf flag & Violets
7. Blue flower in lowgrounds vanished.
11.The purple flag, Dwarf flag, Violet & wild Honeysuckle still in bloom.
Went journey to Maryland, Pennsylva[nia], New York, so observations cease

(page 1, back)
Feb. 20. Sowed a bed of forwardest and a bed of midling peas.
*500. of these peas weighed 3 oz. —18 [dwt.] about 2,500 fill a pint.
Mar. 9. Both beds of peas up.
15. Planted asparagus seed in 5. beds of 4 [ft.] width. 4. rows in each.
17. Sowed a bed of forwardest peas, and a bed of the latest of all.
23. Purple Hyacinth & Narcissus bloom.
Sowed 2 rows of Celery 9 [in.] apart.
Sowed 2 rows of Spanish onions & 2 [do] of Lettuce.
Apr. 1. Peas of Mar. 17 just appearing.
2. Sowed Carnations, Indian pink, Marygold, Globe amaranth, Auricula, Double balsam, Tricolor, Dutch violet, Sensitive plant, Cockscomb, a flower like the Prince's feather, Lathyrus.
Planted Lilac, Spanish broom, Umbrella, Laurel.
Almonds, Muscle plumbs, Cayenne pepper.
12. Cuttings of Gooseberries.
4. Planted suckers of Roses, seeds of Althaea & Prince's feather.
6. Planted lillies & wild honeysuckles.
7. Planted strawberry roots.
9. Sowed 3, rows of Celery, 2 [do] of Lettuce—2 [do] of Radish.
Lunaria in full bloom.
16. Sweet Williams begin to open.
24. Forwardest peas of Feb. 20, come to table.
25. Asparagus 3. inches high, and branched.
Feathered hyacinth in bloom, also Sweet Williams.
A pink in bed VI. c. blooming.
Lunaria still in bloom, an indifferent flower.

(page 2, front)
May. 27. Sowed Lettuce, Radish, Broccoli, & Cauliflower.
28. Flower–de luces just opening.
*Strawberries come to table. Note this is the first year of their bearing having been planted in the spring of 1766. and on an average, the plants bear 20 strawberries each. 100 fill half a pint.
Forwardest peas of March 17 come to table.
Latest peas of Feb. 20 will come to table within about 4 days.
Snap-dragon blooming.
June. 4. Larkspur & Lychnis bloom & Poppies
10. Pinks & Hollyhocks bloom.   by information of Mrs Carr.
12. Carnations bloom.
18. Argemone put out one flower.
July. 5. Larger Poppy has vanished. Dwarf poppy still in bloom but on the decline
pinks V. c. just disappear. Pinks in VI. c. still shew a few.
Carnations in full life —Larkspur, Lychnis in bloom. —a few hollyhocks remaining—Eastern mallow almost vanished, an

indifferent flower.
* Colo Moore tells me a hill of artichokes generally bears 8 of a year, and they continue in season about 6 weeks.
18. Lesser poppy still blooming. Pinks V.c. a few. Pinks VI.c. a few. A few Carnations. Larkspur in bloom. Eastern mallow & Lychnis in bloom. Mirabilis just opened, very clever. Argemone, one flower out, this is the 4th [ys] year.
31. Cucumbers come to table.
Aug. 1. Inoculated May cherry buds into 4 stocks of unknown kind.
2. Inoculated English walnut buds into stocks of the Black walnut.
3. Inoculated common cherry buds into stocks of large kind at Monticello.
Nov. 22 *8 or 10 bundles of fodder are as much as a horse will generally eat thro[ugh] the night
9 bundles X 130 days = 1170 for the winter.

(page 2, back)
1786
Feb. 24. Sowed a patch of early peas, having first soaked them. Charlton Hotspur.
*500. of these peas weighed 3oz. – 7 dwt. 2000 filled a pint accurately.
Mar. 5. Sowed a patch of Spanish Marotto peas.
Mar. 14 Peas of Feb. 24, just appearing.
Mar. 28. Peas of Mar. 5, just appearing.

Page 24
Monticello Dependencies plan

(front)
Fattening room. Chariot-room.
Shop. Laboratory. Lumber-room. Solitudini volum. Office. Bed-chamber.

(back)
Lower story 8 [ft.] pitch will take 56,500 bricks
Upper story 12 [ft.] pitch will take <u>54,500</u>
                                        111,000

In the temp. Cloacinae a Venetian blind before the lower sash, the upper to the let down

Monticello Mountain plan

(front, upper left)
On the S.W. side of the walk towards the grove
17 Wild crabs 25 [ft.] apart, 6 [ft.] from edge of walk.
16 Pride of China beyond them, breaking the rows.
14 Catalpas beyond them
15 Umbrellas beyond them
Aspens beyond them
Walnuts beyond them
Elms beyond them

(front, upper right)
Observations from a [indecipherable] of the mountain back of Monticello. Aug. 4, 1772.
Willis's mountain bore S. 2°. E.
Slate river mountains, highest point S. 29°. W.
Their Eastern end, running low, bore S. 21. W.
Monticello house then bore N. 18°. E.
Observations from Monticello, same day.
Willis's mountain S. 1°. E
Intersection of the back mountain with horizon S. 12°. W.
Dwelling house fronts S. 65°. W & N. 65°. E.
My little Piney mountain bears from N.W. corner of Kitchen S. 33° 45' E. 349 yards
The Slate quarry bears from Monticello S. 32. E.
The mountains seen from Elkhill are from N.77.W. to N.28.W
Elk-hill bears from Monticello S.48.E.
(front, middle)
Radius = 40 [ft.]
Both versed sines = 36 [ft.]
One versed sine = 18 [ft.]
Therefore find the angle whose versed sine is to Radius as 18:40 or 9:20 the sine of that angle doubled will give the length of a.b.
The cosine is = Rad. – versed sine = 40 – 18 = 22
The Sine^2 = Rad.^{2} – Cosine^2 = 1600 – 484 = 1116
Sine = $\sqrt{1116}$ = 33.4
ab = 66.8

(front, bottom middle)
441 [ft.] by actual measuration from where the ellipses intersects the line of [indecipherable] Cherries at each end which admits 19 intervals of 23 [ft.] 2½ [in.] and of course 18 trees
(from left to right)
Persian jasmine
Cape jasmine
Lilac
Euonymus [indecipherable]

Persian Jasmine
Cape jasmine
Daphne
Persian jasmine
Persian jasmine
Daphne
Persian jasmine
Euonymus Latifolia
[indecipherable] lilac
Cape jasmine
Persian jasmine

(front, right)
a.a. Italian Larch
b. Chinese Arborvitae
c. Thuya Occidentals
d.d. N.F. Land spruce
e.e. Balm of gilead fire

This hedge is to range with the trees on the N.G. side of the offices, i.e. its [centre] is to be a line 5 [ft.] from N.E. [indecipherable] well of offices [indecipherable] need another hedge to range with the trees at apart will form one side of an alcove on each side of the house and throw the [ends] passage of offices properly in the [center] between [indecipherable] at 12[ft.] 4 1/2[in.] apart will form one side of each of the alcoves to the N. & S. very over Stable & Laundry & throw the crop [indecipherable] the [indecipherable] trees on the S.E. side of the offices between there two hedges [indecipherable] house to be placed.

(back)
The whole circumference is 3715.88 feet or 1238.62 yards.

Monticello Cellar plan

Plan of the cellar floors.

Underpinning of Portico.

The dotted line is the [indecipherable] of the wall above and consequently [indecipherable] on which side the diminitions.
The diminetion is 9 ½ [ft.] except in the left hand partition wall which has no dimension.
The middle building on the cellar floor is 29 [ft.] 3 [in.] in front, and 35 [ft.] 10 [in.] in flank.
The North west wing is 19 [ft.] 6 [in.] in front, and 25 [ft.] 9 2/10 [in.] in flank.
The South East wing is 19 [ft.] 6 [in.] in front, and 22 [ft.] 6 2/10 [in.] in flank.

Page 27
Monticello Final first-floor plan

Plan of the first floor showing the thickness Etc. of the walls above the water table

(top, right)
17 [ft.] 11 1/3 [in.] to naked of wall of basement.

(rooms, from left to right)
Bed-room. Dressing-room. Parlour. Dining-room. North Bow-room.
Antichamber. Lodge. Stairs.

(bottom, left)
The middle building from outside to out-side is 28 [ft.] 6 [in.] by 44 [ft.] 7 8/10 [in.]
The wings detached from middle building 9 [ft.] 6 [in.] by *21 [ft.] 9 2/10 [in.]
An Intercolonnation is 7 [ft.] .8991666 [in.]
From center to center of column is 9 [ft.] 0.89075 [in.]
The diminetion of the wall of the Ionic or upper story 1.436965 [in.] externally and if from that diminetion it can fall back from the perpendicular 1.299265 [in.] just as the Ionic column does, the entablature of the house will be brought to range perfectly with that of the Ionic column.
*On measuring, this turns out but 21 [ft.] 6 [in.]

(bottom, right)
The upper wall of the middle building must diminish externally 3 7/8 of the Ionic column that its entablature may answer to that of the columns, this being half the diminetion of the Ionic column, the flank of the Doric pilaster must for the same reason, project half its diminetion, that is 3 3/5 = 1.43695 [in.] beyond the surface of the wall. Projection of portico from the wall. Pilaster........................10' = 0 [ft.] 3.83193 [in.]

From front of pilaster to front of column 9 [ft.] 0.89075 [in.]
Projection of base of column.........10' 0 [ft.] 3.83193 [in.]
9 [ft.] 8.55461 [in.]

From the center of the window of the Lodge to one of the middle pilasters is 3 [ft.] 0.45385 [in.]
Subtract half the window 5 [ft.] 7 ½ [in.] + the architecture 6 ½ [in.] .... 2 [ft.] 2 [in.]
It leaves ....10.45385 [in.]
Subtract from that the projection of the external pediment of the window ...... 7.4285 [in.]
It leaves the space between that projection and the pilaster, to wi[dth],   3.02535 [in.]
It shows therefore the two middle pilasters on that side of the house will [indecipherable] the [pediments] of [windows]

Page 30
Monticello Tower plan

(left)
The columns to be nothing but planks cut for a mould of the order.
The entablature to be a plain plank with the projections of the order cut at the end. No entablature but in the front.
A window in the center of each order, to be in the back as well as front. The front window to be as much lowest as to direct the line of sight to Monticello.
The interstices of the wall to be filled up with stone without mortar.
The diminetions of the wall to be all on the outside.

(right)
Corrigenda
Give a basement to the lower [indecipherable]
There should be a basement on the pediment on which the Doric should be erected.
The wall should be counted from outside to out-side of pillar in proportioning it to the height, [if] not from inside to inside as in this draught.
The outside of the column should be plumb of the naked of the wall of the next order below.
The space between the wall & column should be a proper intercolonnation [of] 1 1/2 diam.
The Composite should be an Octagon with arches like Cobb's designs Pl.31 fig.2.

Page 36
Letter to Anne Randolph, June 7, 1707

Washington June 7. 07.

My dear Anna,
I received last week from your papa information that you were all well except your mama, who had still some remains of the pain in the face. I hope I shall hear this week that she also is restored to her health. From yourself I may soon expect a report of your first visit to Monticello, and of the state of our joint concerns there. I find that the limited number of our flower beds will too much restrain the variety of flowers in which we might wish to indulge, & therefore I have resumed an idea, which I had formerly entertained, but had laid by, of a winding walk surrounding the lawn before the house, with a narrow border of flowers on each side, this would give us abundant room for a great variety. I enclose you a sketch of my idea, where the dotted lines on each side of the black line shew the border on each side of the walk, the hollows of the walk would give room for oval beds of flowering shrubs. Will you tell your papa that Joseph has put into my hands Marmontel's memoir, and 7 Dollars being the surplus of money left after paying Duane's account. The 7 Dollars are included in a [remittance] I now make to Mr. Bacon, who is instructed to deliver them to Mr. Randolph. The books making too large a packet for the [port], I shall reserve them to bring with one, unless some earlier [usury] once offers. Kiss your dear Mama and the young ones for me. Present me affectionately to your Papa, and accept the assurances of my love for yourself.

Thomas Jefferson

Page 44
Letter to James Madison, September 20, 1785

Paris   Sep. 20, 1785

Dear Sir,

By Mr. Fitzhugh, you will receive my letter of the first instant. He is still here, and gives me an opportunity of again addressing you much sooner than I should have done, but for the discovery of a great piece of inattention. In that letter I send you a detail of the cost of your books, and desire you to keep the amount in your hands, as if I had forgot that a part of it was in fact your own, as being a balance of what I had remained in your debt. I really did not attend to it in the moment of writing, and when it occurred to me, I revised my memorandum book from the time of our being in Philadelphia together, and stated our account from the beginning, lest I should forget or mistake any part of it. I enclose you this statement. You will always be so good as to let me know, from time to time, your advances for me. Correct with freedom all my proceedings for you, as, in what I do, I have no other desire than that of doing exactly what will be most pleasing to you.

I received this summer a letter from Messrs. Buchanan and Hay, as Directors of the public buildings, desiring I would have drawn for them, plans of sundry buildings, and, in the first place, of a capitol. They fixed, for their receiving this plan, a day which was within about six weeks of that on which their letter came to my hand. I engaged an architect of capital abilities in this business. Much time was requisite, after the external form was agreed on, to make the internal distribution convenient for the three branches of government. This time was much lengthened by my avocations to other objects, which I had no right to neglect. The plan however was settled. The gentlemen had sent me one which they had thought of. The one agreed on here, is more convenient, more beautiful, gives more room, and will not cost more than two thirds of what that would. We took for our model what is called the Maison quarree of [Nimes], one of the most beautiful, if not the most beautiful and precious morsel of architecture left us by antiquity. It was built by Caius and Lucius Caesar, and repaired by Louis XIV., and has the suffrage of all the judges of architecture, who have seen it, as yielding to no one of the beautiful monuments of Greece, Rome, Palmyra, and Balbec, which late travellers have communicated to us. It is very simple, but it is noble beyond expression, and would have done honor to our country, as presenting to travellers a specimen of taste in our infancy, promising much for our maturer age. I have been much mortified with information, which I received two days ago from Virginia, that the first brick of the capitol would be laid within a few days. But surely, the delay of this piece of a summer would have been repaired by the savings in the plan preparing here, were we to value its other superiorities as nothing. But how is a taste in this beautiful art to be formed in our countrymen, unless we avail ourselves of every occasion when public buildings are to be erected, of presenting to them models for their study and imitation? Pray try if you can effect the stopping of this work. I have written also to E. R. on the subject. The loss will be only of the laying the bricks already laid, or a part of them. The bricks themselves will do again for the interior walls, and one side wall and one end wall may remain, as they will answer equally well for our plan. This loss is not to be weighed against the saving of money which will arise, against the comfort of laying out the public money for something honorable, the satisfaction of seeing an object and proof of national good taste, and the regret and mortification of erecting a monument of our barbarism, which will be loaded with execrations as long as it shall endure. The plans are in good forwardness, and I hope will be ready within three or four weeks. They could not be stopped now, but on paying their whole price, which will be considerable. If the undertakers are afraid to undo what they have done, encourage them to it by a recommendation from the Assembly. You see I am an enthusiast on the subject of the arts. But it is an enthusiasm of which I am not ashamed, as its object is to improve the taste of my countrymen, to increase their reputation, to reconcile to them the respect of the world, and procure them its praise.

I shall send off your books, in two trunks, to Havre, within two or three days, to the care of Mr. Limozin, American agent there. I will advise you, as soon as I know by what vessel he forwards them. Adieu.

Yours affectionately,
Thomas Jefferson

Page 58
Poplar Forest survey

(clockwise from top)

[fountains] on the entry line on the land

S 31 W [symbol] 68 poles to new line

Red Oak Near the path

S 49 W 80/20 New Line
Lowest
S 57 W [symbol] 10 poles to Calloway's old line

A Calloway Corner Red O in a branch
down the branch to the beginning
S 70 W 66 fro to [pointers] in the branch

[indecipherable] Oak

N 7 [symbol] 200 poles to N 4 [symbols] poles to
Along Calloway's [line] to
[pointers] to the Cal[loway's Corner]

[Spanish] Oak

New lines N 74 [symbol] 33[4] poles to

[pointers] on the entry line
S 13 [symbol] 1 [symbols]
Chestnut

S 70 [symbol] 59 fro

Page 62
Letter to Benjamin Rush, August 17, 1811

Poplar Forest, Aug. 17, 1811.

Dear Sir,

I write to you from a place ninety miles from Monticello, near the new London of this State, which I visit three or four times a year, and stay from a fortnight to a month at a time. I have fixed myself comfortably, keep some books here, bring others occasionally, am in the solitude of a hermit, and quite at leisure to attend to my absent friends. I note this to show that I am not in a situation to examine the dates of our letters, whether I have overgone the annual period of asking how you do? I know that within that time I have received one or more letters from you, accompanied by a volume of your introductory lectures, for which accept my thanks. I have read them with pleasure and edification, for I acknowledge facts in medicine as far as they go, distrusting only their extension by theory. Having to conduct my grandson through his course of mathematics, I have resumed that study with great avidity. It was ever my favorite one. We have no theories there, no uncertainties remain on the mind; all is demonstration and satisfaction. I have forgotten much, and recover it with more difficulty than when in the vigor of my mind I originally acquired it. It is wonderful to me that old men should not be sensible that their minds keep pace with their bodies in the progress of decay. Our old revolutionary friend Clinton, for example, who was a hero, but never a man of mind, is wonderfully jealous on this head. He tells eternally the stories of his younger days to prove his memory, as if memory and reason were the same faculty. Nothing betrays imbecility so much as the being insensible of it. Had not a

conviction of the danger to which an unlimited occupation of the executive chair would expose the republican constitution of our government, made it conscientiously a duty to retire when I did, the fear of becoming a dotard and of being insensible of it, would of itself have resisted all solicitations to remain. I have had a long attack of rheumatism, without fever and without pain while I keep myself still. A total prostration of the muscles of the back, hips and thighs, deprived me of the power of walking, and leaves it still in a very impaired state. A pain when I walk, seems to have fixed itself in the hip, and to threaten permanence. I take moderate rides, without much fatigue; but my journey to this place, in a hard-going gig, gave me great sufferings which I expect will be renewed on my return as soon as I am able. The loss of the power of taking exercise would be a sore affliction to me. It has been the delight of my retirement to be in constant bodily activity, looking after my affairs. It was never damped as the pleasures of reading are, by the question of cui bono? for what object? I hope your health of body continues firm. Your works show that of your mind. The habits of exercise which your calling has given to both, will tend long to preserve them. The sedentary character of my public occupations sapped a constitution naturally sound and vigorous, and draws it to an earlier close. But it will still last quite as long as I wish it. There is a fulness of time when men should go, and not occupy too long the ground to which others have a right to advance. We must continue while here to exchange occasionally our mutual good wishes. I find friendship to be like wine, raw when new, ripened with age, the true old man's milk and restorative cordial. God bless you and preserve you through a long and healthy old age.

Thomas Jefferson

Page 62
Poplar Forest Kitchen plan

From the foundation to the water table 2 [ft.] thick, & 5 [ft.] high, sinking 2 [ft.] into the ground.
From the water table to the bottom of the joists 18 [in.] thick & 10 feet high.
Doors to be 3 [ft.] 10[in.] opening in the stone work, which admits a door 3 [ft.] 6 [in.] and 2 [in.] on each side for facing 7 [ft.] 2 [in.]
Opening in height, which admits a door 7 [ft.] high and 2 [in.] [indecipherable]
Windows to be 2 [ft.] 6 [in.] from the floor, 4 [ft.] 4 [in.] width of opening, and 7 [ft.] 4 [in.] height of [symbol]. In the stone work, which admits windows of 3 [ft.] 3 [in.] by 6 [ft.] 6 [in.] clear, an architrave at top & on each side of 6 ½ [in.] and a sill of 3 ½ [in.]
The windows [inlay] 6 [in.] on each side within.
The fire places 2 [ft.] deep, 2 [ft.] wide in the back and 5 [ft.] wide in front.
The joists to project 11 Inches.
The roof to be hipped at each end, the height of it at the ridge pole 6 [ft.] to be sheeted, and shingled. The shingles to be joisted.
The mortar to be one third lime and two thirds clean sand without any loam.
The shaft of the chimney to be of brick, to come out exactly in the middle every way, to be 3 [ft.] by 2 [ft.] outside
The flues to be 12 by 16 [in.] with a partition between of half a brick thickness.
The North room to be filled up to the floor with earth, & to be paved with brick. The South room to be plank floor.
The foundation being 6 [in.] thicker than the wall above, leaves 3 [in.] projection inside for the sleepers to rest on.
The ends of the house are to look to the North & South, the sides to the East and West.
Having driven a [trim] in the center of the spot destined for a dwelling house hereafter, measure 50 [ft.] due East from that trim, and there make the center of the door as at a.

Page 76
UVA Rotunda Floor 1

(left)
Breadth of Portico 16 = 46
[indecipherable] of Dome 11 [ft.]
[indecipherable] of [indecipherable] 8 [ft.]
19 [ft.]

(right)
The height of the wall within, to the spring of the [indecipherable]) the diameter must 1-6
They are arranged must be 27 [ft.] (or [indecipherable] diam.) circumference 113 diameter = 169
To correspond with the windows there must be 20. intercolonnations.
And that the intercolonnation may not be too [large] for the Corinthian order we
An intercolonnation of 3. diameter will be 4-6
2 columns …………………………………3-
Space between them 40. ………………… 1-
8-6 x 20 = 170

UVA Rotunda Floor 2
Rotunda, reduced to the proportions of the Pantheon and accommodated to the purposes of a Library for the University with rooms for drawing, music, examinations and other accessory purposes.
The diameter of the building 77. Feet, being 1/2 that of the Pantheon, consequently 1/4 A, area, & 1/8 A, volume. The Circumference 242 [ft.]

Page 78
Letter to Dr. William Thornton, May 9, 1817

Monticello May 9, 17.
Dear Sir,
Your favor of Apr 18 was duly received, and the two drawings were delivered here by Mr. and Mrs. Madison in perfect good order. With respect to Cirrachhi's bust, any artist whom you may dispose to do so shall be welcome to come and make a cast of plaister form it. We have always plaister at had.
We are commencing here the establishment of a college, and instead of building a magnificent house which would exhaust all our funds, we propose to lay off a square of about 7 or 800 [ft.] on the outside of which we shall arrange separate

pavilions, one for each professor and his scholars. each pavilion will have a schoolroom below, and 2 rooms for the Professor above and between pavilion and pavilion a range of dormitories for the boys, one story high, giving each a room 10 [ft.] wide & 14 [ft.] deep. The pavilions about 36 [ft.] wide in front and 24 [ft.] in depth. This sketch will give you an idea of it.

[sketch] "grass & trees"

The whole of the pavilions and dormitories to be united by a colonnade in front, of the height of the lower story of the pavilions, under which they may go dry from school to school. the colonnade will be of square brick pilasters (at first) with a Tuscan entablature. Now what we wish is that these pavilions as they will show themselves above the dormitories shall be models of taste & good architecture, and of a variety of appearance, no two alike, so as to serve as specimens for the architectural lectures. Will you set your imagination to work & sketch some designs for us, no matter how loosely with (letter continues on back) the pen, without the trouble of referring to scale or rule; for we want nothing but the outline of the architecture, as the internal must be arranged according to local convenience. A few sketches, such as need not take you a moment, will greatly oblige us. The Visitors of the College are President Monroe, Mr. Madison, 3 others whom you do not know & myself. We have to struggle against two important wants, money, and men for professors capable of fulfilling our views. They may come in time for all Europe seems to be breaking up. In the meantime help us to provide snug and handsome lodges for them. I salute you with friendship and respect.

Thomas Jefferson

Page 80
UVA Pavilion and Dormitories plan

(front, top right)
There is an error in this Chinese [indecipherable]
The panels showed have been from [indecipherable]as is seen in the Pavilion

The pilasters in front of the [Pavilion] are erroneously planed. The [indecipherable] should be opposite the corners of the inner should be equally distanced before them.

(front, center)
alcove

(back, left)
257 yards

(back, right)
The walls of the Pavilion are 116 [ft.] running measure.
Cellar 2 bricks thick, 10 [ft.] high, 24 bricks to a square foot. 24 x 10 x 116 amount to 27,860 27[810]
   26
Upper walls 23 [ft.] high, 1 ½ brick thick, 18 bricks to a square foot. 18 x 23 x 116 ... 48, 024 say 53,3[60]
The chimney ... 4,752 ... 4,7[8]2
6 pilasters ... 1,134 1,134
   81,750 bricks 87,086
The [necessary] Appendix, passage [symbol] (61 [ft.] runs measure, 9 [ft.] high, 1 brick thick) 6,588

Each Chamber has 36 [ft.] of wall, running measure.
If 10 [ft.] high and 1 brick thick, 10 x 12 x 36 amount to 4,320 bricks
One half of the chimney (one chimney serving 2 chambers) 656
2 pilasters ... 270
But if the walls be 1 ½ br[ick] thick there must be added 5,246
   2,160
   7,406
20 chambers to each pavilion therefore will require ... 104,920 bricks or 14 [8,120]
And a Pavilion with its 20 chambers will take ... 192,258 or 235, [688]

The method of making a rough estimate in Philadelphia, of the cost of a brick dwelling house, finished in a plain way, is to reckon the carpenter's <u>work</u> equal to the cost of the brick walls, and the carpenter's <u>materials</u> and the [iron masonry] equal also to the cost of the brick walls. But in the present case, the carpenter's materials (timber) will either be given, or cost very little, and the [iron masonry] will be little. I believe therefore the cost of the carpenter's materials and [iron masonry] need not be stated at more than half the cost of the brick walls, reckoning brickwork therefore at 10 [symbol] the thousand, the cost may be roughly estimated as follows.

D[ollars] C[ents]	D C		D C D C
Pavilion walls 817.50 Carpenter's work 817.50 Carpenter's materials and [iron masonry]			408.75 = [2,043.75]
Appendix on the same principles ...			167.70

D   C
Chambers each on the same principles costing 131.15, 20 chambers will cost ... 2623.
The establishment of a Pavilioin and 20 chambers for each professorship will cost therefore 4831.45

The estimate above is made on the supposition that each Professor with his pupils (suppose 20) shall have a separate Pavilion of 26 by 34 [ft.] outside, and 24 by 32 inside measure in which the ground floor (of 12 [ft.] pitch clear) is to be the schoolroom,
   13
and 2 rooms above (10 [ft.] pitch clear) and a kitchen below (7 [ft.] pitch clear) for the use of the Professor. On each side of the Pavilion are to be 10 chambers, 10 by 14 [ft.] in the clear and 8 [ft.] pitch, with a fireplace in each, for the students. The whole to communic[able] by a colonnade of 8 [ft.] width in the clear. The pilasters of brick to be generally 5 ½ [ft.] apart from center to center.
   The kitchen will be 24 by 14 on the back of the building adjacent to the chimney, with 2 windows looking back. The cellar 24 by 10 also, on the front side, with 2 windows looking into the colonnade. The Pavilions fronting South should have their staircase on the East; those fronting East or West should have the stairs at the North side of the building, that the windows may open to the pleasant[est] Greens.

Backyards, gardens, stables, [horses] [symbol] to be in the grounds adjacent to the Square, on the outside.

UVA Pavilion I elevation

(front)
[No. I] Pavilion West

(back)
No. I of the Doric of Diocletian [boths] Chambray
Front of the building 44 [ft.] height from the zocle 27 7.65
Diam[eter] of column 2 ~ 9' = .55 a [metop] and [triglyph] 3 ~ 5.25 = 41.25 projection of the
Cornice 48 = 26.4
Height of the column 8 ~ 0' = 22.0
Entabl[ature] [indecipherable] archit[ecture] 32' = 1 ~ 5.6

Diam.	Frise	45' =	2 ~ 0.75	5 ~ 7.65
1-53	Cornice	46' =	2 ~1.3	
Order entire		10 ~ 3 =	27 ~ 7.65	

   diam. diam.
44 [ft.] front admist 4 column of 2.9 and 3 intercol[omns] of 4 or 16 = 44
   1 ~ 4.5 + 13 ~ 9 + 13 ~ 9 + 1 ~ 4.5 = 44
A door in the center of the middle intercollonation, and a window in the center of each of the others.
Consequently, thus space 8 ~ 3 + 13 ~ 9 + 13 ~ 9 + 8 ~ 3 = 44 [ft.]
The whole height from the zocle being 27 ~ 7.65
The upper joists are above and upon the Cornice.
Middle [symbol] 1
Floor above the zocle 2
Leaving 24 ~ 7.65 for clear width of 2 rooms
   27 ~ 7.65
Let the upper room then be clear 12 ~ 9
The lower ... clear 11 ~ 10.65
   24 ~ 7.65
It will then be exterior entablature ... 5 ~ 7.65 12 ~ 9
Between bottom of entablature and floor 7 ~ 1.35
Middle joists, floor and ceiling ... 1 ~
Clear pitch of lower rooms ... 11 ~ 10.65
From the lower floor to the zocle a descent by steps of 2
   27 ~ 7.65

From the zocle to the upper floor ...

   14 ~ 10.65
The Tuscan order of the colonnade ... 11 ~ 7.86 = 15 ~
   Requiring steps of descent from the upper floor to the [terras] of the Dormitories 3 ~ 2.79
From the ceiling of the kitchen to the level of the zocle is 1 [ft.]
   From the level of the zocle to the floor of the kitchen 7 making clear pitch of kitchen 8 [ft.]
   To the bottom of the foundation ... 2 making the depth of the wall below the [indecipherable] 9 [ft.]

IMAGE CREDITS

Slipcase cover: (clockwise from top left): Bettmann/Corbis; Courtesy of Massachusetts Historical Society; Courtesy of Massachusetts Historical Society; Monticello/Thomas Jefferson Foundation, Inc.; The Granger Collection, New York; Courtesy of Massachusetts Historical Society; Courtesy of Massachusetts Historical Society

Book front cover: Special Collections, University of Virginia Library

Book back cover: Special Collections, University of Virginia Library

Book spine: Bettmann/Corbis

Title page: Bettmann/Corbis

Page 2: Special Collections, University of Virginia Library

Page 4-5: Kean Collection/Getty Images

Page 7: Joseph Sohm/Visions of America/Corbis

Page 8: Library of Congress; (inset) Hulton Archive/Getty Images

Page 10: Hannah Verdi Warfield/Tuckahoe Plantation

Page 11: Hannah Verdi Warfield/Tuckahoe Plantation

Page 12: Library of Congress

Page 13: Library of Congress

Page 14: Bettmann/Corbis; (flap, front) Library of Congress

Page 15: Yann Arthus-Bertrand/Corbis

Page 16: Andrea Palladio

Page 17: Library of Congress

Page 18: (enclosures) Courtesy of Massachusetts Historical Society

Page 19: Monticello/Thomas Jefferson Foundation, Inc.

Page 20: Paul J. Richards/AFP/Getty Images; (inset) Bettmann/Corbis

Page 22: Library of Congress; (flap, front) Monticello/Thomas Jefferson Foundation, Inc.; (flap, back) Library of Congress

Page 23: Special Collections, University of Virginia Library

Page 24: Monticello/Thomas Jefferson Foundation, Inc.; (enclosures) Courtesy of Massachusetts Historical Society

Page 25: Library of Congress

Page 26: Bettmann/Corbis

Page 27: Courtesy of Massachusetts Historical Society

Page 28: Courtesy of Massachusetts Historical Society

Page 29: Monticello/Thomas Jefferson Foundation, Inc.; (background) Courtesy of Massachusetts Historical Society

Page 30: Tim Wright/Corbis; (enclosures) Courtesy of Massachusetts Historical Society

Page 31: Courtesy of Massachusetts Historical Society

Page 32: Courtesy of Massachusetts Historical Society; (flap) Courtesy of Massachusetts Historical Society

Page 33: The Granger Collection, New York

Page 34: Monticello/Thomas Jefferson Foundation, Inc.

Page 35: Monticello/Thomas Jefferson Foundation, Inc.

Page 36: (flap) David Muench/Corbis; (insert) Courtesy of Massachusetts Historical Society

Page 37: (top) Courtesy of Massachusetts Historical Society; (bottom) Monticello/Thomas Jefferson Foundation, Inc.

Page 38: Monticello/Thomas Jefferson Foundation, Inc.

Page 39: (top) Monticello/Thomas Jefferson Foundation, Inc; (bottom) Library of Congress

Page 41: Medford Taylor/National Geographic/Getty Images

Page 42: Corbis; (inset) Stock Montage/Getty Images

Page 44: Emmet Collection, Miriam and Ira D. Wallach Division of Art, Prints and Photographs, The New York Public Library, Astor, Lenox and Tilden Foundations; (insert) Papers of Thomas Jefferson, Manuscripts Division, Library of Congress

Page 45: David Muench/Corbis

Page 46: Andrea Palladio

Page 47: The Gallery Collection/Corbis

Page 48: Courtesy of Massachusetts Historical Society; (enclosures) Courtesy of Massachusetts Historical Society

Page 49: Library of Congress

Page 50: Library of Virginia

Page 51: Corbis

Page 52: Library of Congress

Page 53: Library of Congress

Page 54: AP Photo/Steve Helber

Page 55: Henry Groskinsky/Time Life Pictures/Getty Images

Page 56: Library of Congress

Page 58: Courtesy of Massachusetts Historical Society

Page 59: (flap) Library of Congress; (insert and background) Courtesy of Massachusetts Historical Society

Page 60: Library of Congress

Page 61: Library of Congress

Page 62: Library of Congress; (enclosures, plans) Courtesy of Massachusetts Historical Society; (enclosures, letter) Papers of Thomas Jefferson, Manuscripts Division, Library of Congress

Page 63: Library of Congress

Page 64: Monticello/Thomas Jefferson Foundation, Inc.

Page 65: Courtesy of Thomas Jefferson's Poplar Forest, Les Schofer, photographer

Page 66: Library of Congress

Page 68: Library of Virginia; (inset) Monticello/Thomas Jefferson Foundation, Inc.

Page 70: Emmet Collection, Miriam and Ira D. Wallach Division of Art, Prints and Photographs, The New York Public Library, Astor, Lenox and Tilden Foundations

Page 71: White House Historical Association (White House Collection)

Page 72: I.N. Phelps Stokes Collection, Miriam and Ira D. Wallach Division of Art, Prints and Photographs, The New York Public Library, Astor, Lenox and Tilden Foundations; (background) Special Collections, University of Virginia Library; (flap, front) Courtesy of Massachusetts Historical Society

Page 73: I.N. Phelps Stokes Collection, Miriam and Ira D. Wallach Division of Art, Prints and Photographs, The New York Public Library, Astor, Lenox and Tilden Foundations

Page 74: Library of Congress; (flap, front) Corbis; (flap, back) Courtesy of Adam P. Fagen via Flickr.com

Page 75: Buddy Mays/Corbis

Page 76: iStock/Bill Manning; (enclosures) Special Collections, University of Virginia Library

Page 77: Library of Congress

Page 78: Special Collections, University of Virginia Library

Page 79: Library of Virginia

Page 80: Library of Congress; (enclosures) Special Collections, University of Virginia Library

Page 81: Michael Freeman/Corbis

Page 82: Special Collections, University of Virginia Library

Page 83: Richard T. Nowitz/Corbis

Page 84: iStock/John Weise

Page 85: Tim Wright/Corbis

BIBLIOGRAPHY

Brodie, Fawn. *Thomas Jefferson: An Intimate History*. New York: W. W. Norton & Co., 1974.

The Colonial Williamsburg Foundation, 2007. *Tour the Town*. http://www.colonialwilliamsburg.com/visit/tourTheTown/.

The Corporation for Jefferson's Poplar Forest, 2007. *Thomas Jefferson the Architect*. http://www.poplarforest.org/tjarchitecture.html.

Ellis, Joseph. *American Sphinx: The Character of Thomas Jefferson*. New York: Knopf, 1996.

Hitchens, Christopher. *Thomas Jefferson: Author of America*. New York: HarperCollins Eminent Lives, 2005.

Howard, Hugh. *Dr. Kimball and Mr. Jefferson: Rediscovering the Founders of American Architecture*. New York: Bloomsbury USA, 2006.

—. *Thomas Jefferson, Architect: The Built Legacy of Our Third President*. New York: Rizzoli International Publications, 2003.

Malone, Dumas. *Jefferson and His Times* (six volumes). First volumes published by Little, Brown & Co.

The Massachusetts Historical Society, 2003. *The Thomas Jefferson Papers: An Electronic Archive*. http://www.masshist.org/thomasjeffersonpapers/.

Peterson, Merrill. *Thomas Jefferson and the New Nation*. New York: Oxford University Press, 1970.

Randall, Willard Sterne. *Thomas Jefferson: A Life*. New York: Henry Holt & Co., 1993.

The Rector and Visitors of the University of Virginia, 2007. *Thomas Jefferson's Academical Village*. http://www.virginia.edu/academicalvillage/.

The Thomas Jefferson Foundation, 2005. *Monticello Explorer*. http://explorer.monticello.org/index.html.

The Virginia General Assembly, 2005-2007. Capitol Building. http://legis.state.va.us/1_vis_guide/cap_building.html.

ABOUT THE AUTHOR

Chuck Wills has worked as a writer and editor for more than twenty years, serving as an editorial director for DK Publishing, Inc., and international and co-editions editor for Rodale Books International. He has written or contributed to many books on American history. As a writer, his recent books include *Destination America* (DK Publishing, September 2007), a history of immigration to the United States (published in 2005 as a companion volume to the PBS series of the same name), *America's Presidents: Facts, Photos, and Memorabilia from the Nation's Chief Executives* (Thomas Nelson, March 2007), and *Lincoln: The Presidential Archives* (DK Publishing, September 2007).

10 9 8 7 6 5 4 3 2 1

ISBN-13: 978-0-7624-3438-1

Library of Congress Control Number: 2008924844

Thomas Jefferson, Architect: The Interactive Portfolio is produced by
becker&mayer! Books, Bellevue, Washington.
www.beckermayer.com

Design: Kasey Free
Editorial: Amelia Riedler and Jenna Free
Image Research: Chris Campbell
Production Coordination: Leah Finger and Diana Ray

Running Press
2300 Chestnut Street
Philadelphia, PA 19103

Visit us on the Web!
www.runningpress.com